Version Control with Git

From Basics to Expert Proficiency

Contents

Introduction

Version control is an essential component of modern software development, enabling teams to manage changes to their source code over time. It is a system that records changes to a file or set of files so that a specific version can be recalled later. By employing a version control system (VCS), developers can collaborate effectively, maintain a complete history of their work, and safeguard their projects against unexpected issues.

Git, one of the most popular version control systems, has revolutionized the way developers manage and track changes in their codebases. Created by Linus Torvalds in 2005, Git's distributed nature and robust set of features have made it the go-to solution for version control. This book is designed to take you from the basics of version control to expert proficiency with Git.

Understanding version control begins with recognizing its importance in the development process. Version control systems allow multiple developers to work on the same project without overwriting each other's changes. They provide a comprehensive history of all modifications, enabling you to trace back through the development process, compare changes, and revert to previous states if necessary. This historical perspective is invaluable for debugging and ensuring the quality of the software.

The evolution of version control systems has brought about significant improvements in how developers manage their code. Early systems, known as local version control, were limited to individual developers' local machines. Centralized version control systems (CVCS) then emerged, allowing collaboration by storing the versioned files in a central server. However, these systems had their own limitations, primarily the single point of failure. The advent of distributed version control systems (DVCS), such as Git, addressed these issues by providing each developer with a full copy of the project history, promoting redundancy and resilience.

Centralized and distributed version control systems represent two primary approaches to managing code repositories. A CVCS stores all versions of a project in a central repository, with developers checking out and committing changes to this central location. This approach ensures that the repository is always up-to-date but can lead to bottlenecks and potential downtimes if the server fails. In contrast, a DVCS like Git allows each developer to have a complete copy of the repository, enabling offline work and collaboration through multiple distributed repositories. Changes are shared between repositories, and the system handles merging and conflict resolution.

Adopting a version control system offers numerous benefits to development teams. It facilitates parallel development, as multiple developers can work on different features or fixes concurrently. It enhances code quality through code reviews and historical analysis. Additionally, version control provides disaster recovery by allowing you to revert to a previous working state in case of accidental changes or data loss. It also simplifies collaboration by integrating with various development tools and platforms.

Key concepts and terminology form the foundation of version control systems. Terms such as repository, commit, branch, merge, and conflict resolution are fundamental to understanding how Git and other VCS operate. A repository is the storage location for your project's files and history. A commit represents a snapshot of your project at a particular point in time. Branches allow you to work on separate features or fixes in isolation, and merging combines changes from different branches. Conflict resolution is the process of reconciling divergent changes in your code.

Version control systems are employed in various common use cases and scenarios. They are indispensable for software development, documentation, configuration management, and more. In open-source projects, version control allows for transparent and collaborative development, enabling contributions from a global community of developers. In enterprise environments, version control ensures that development processes are repeatable, auditable, and secure.

This book covers the key areas of version control with Git, guiding you through the essential concepts, basic operations, branching and merging, and collaboration workflows. It also delves into advanced techniques, Git hooks and automation, troubleshooting, and best practices.

By the end of this book, you will have a comprehensive understanding of Git and be equipped with the knowledge to utilize its powerful features effectively.

As you embark on this journey of mastering version control with Git, you will gain valuable skills that will enhance your development process, improve collaboration within your team, and contribute to the success of your projects. Welcome to the world of version control with Git.

Chapter 1

Introduction to Version Control

Version control systems are vital tools in software development, enabling teams to manage changes in their codebase efficiently. This chapter covers the fundamental aspects of version control, including its definition, history, and evolution. It compares different types of version control systems, highlighting the differences between centralized and distributed models. The chapter also underscores the benefits of adopting version control systems and explains key concepts and terminology essential for understanding their operation. Common use cases and scenarios where version control systems are employed are also discussed.

1.1 What is Version Control?

Version control, also known as source control or revision control, refers to the process of managing changes to documents, computer programs, large web sites, and other collections of information. This system facilitates the systematic tracking of versions of software or documents over time. The primary purpose of version control is to ensure that all changes are tracked, allowing multiple users to collaborate efficiently and preserving the history of changes for review and rollback purposes.

Version control systems (VCS) are tools designed to help track, manage, and store changes to files. These tools record all modifications to a file or set of files over time so that specific versions can be recalled later, facilitating collaboration and enhancing productivity.

One of the fundamental principles underlying version control is the concept of a repository. The repository, often referred to as the repo, serves as the central data store where all versions of a project's files are maintained. It allows users to add, modify, delete files, and also merge changes made by different contributors.

A version, or revision, is a snapshot of a file or set of files at a particular point in time. Each time a file is saved in the repository, it is assigned a unique revision number or identifier that distinguishes it from other revisions. Users can revert to previous versions if necessary, thereby preventing the loss of work and facilitating the resolution of conflicts.

The basic operations provided by version control systems include:

- **Commit:** The action of saving changes to the repository. A commit operation packages a set of changes into a new revision.
- **Update or Checkout:** The process of retrieving the latest version of a file from the repository.
- **Merge:** The procedure of integrating changes from different sources into a unified version.
- **Branch:** Creating a diverging path within a project to allow for development isolated from the main line of development.
- **Tag:** Marking a specific point in history as important. Typically used for marking release points.

For better illustration, below is an example of the typical workflow using Git, a widely-used version control system. Let's consider a scenario where a user named Alice is working on a file named project.txt:

```
# Initialize a new Git repository
git init

# Add the file to the staging area
git add project.txt

# Commit the file to the repository
git commit -m "Initial commit of project.txt"

# Make a change to the file
echo "New line of text" >> project.txt
```

```
# Add the modified file to the staging area
git add project.txt

# Commit the changes to the repository
git commit -m "Added a new line of text to project.txt"
```

The first command initializes a new Git repository, setting up the necessary metadata. The subsequent git add command stages the file for commit, marking it as ready to be saved in the repository. The git commit command then records the snapshot of the file in its current state, creating a new revision.

To view the history of commits and examine the changes made over time, Alice can use:

```
# Show the commit history
git log
```

This command displays a record of all commits, providing details such as the commit identifier, author, date, and commit message.

Beyond individual file tracking, version control systems also support collaboration among multiple users. When multiple contributors are involved, branches and merge operations become essential. A branch allows developers to diverge from the main project timeline and work independently on features or bug fixes. Merging incorporates changes from different branches back into the main line of development, necessitating conflict resolution when multiple modifications touch the same parts of files.

In contrast to traditional project management methods, version control systems maintain a detailed audit trail, fostering accountability and transparency. Each contributor's changes are tracked and attributed to their respective users, providing a clear history of the project's evolution.

Through the use of version control, teams can reduce the risk of overwriting each other's work, streamline concurrent development, and ensure that the project's history is meticulously recorded, making it an indispensable tool in modern software development practices.

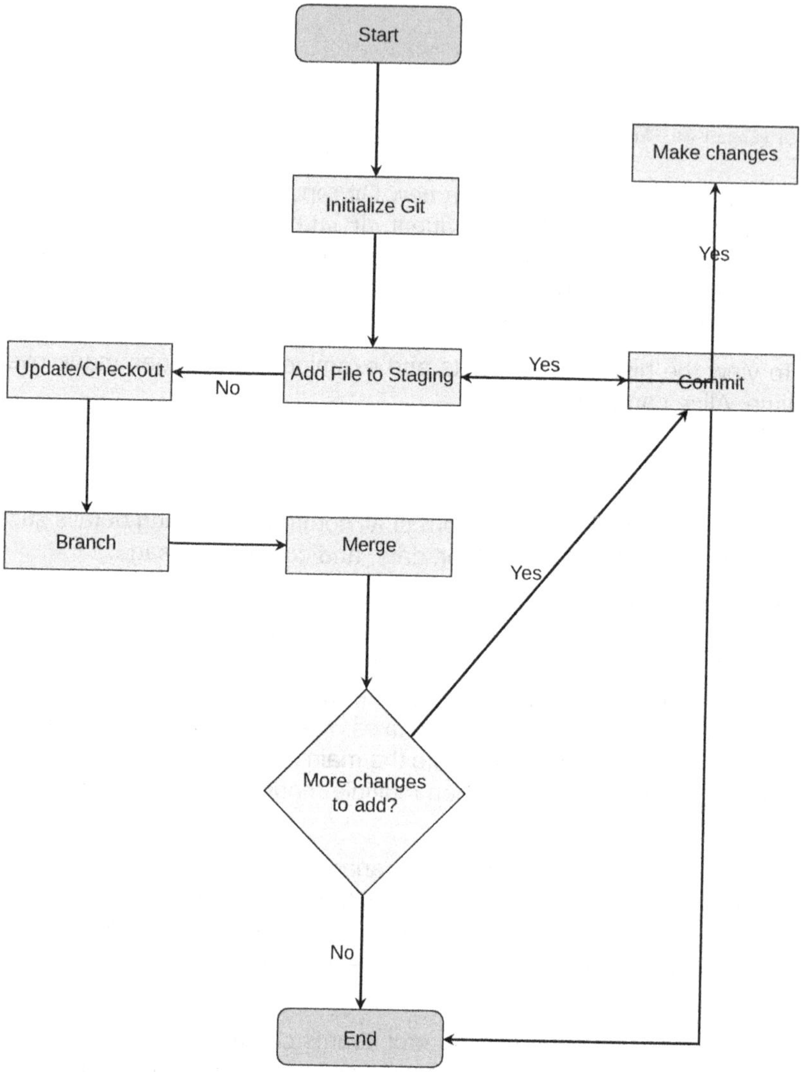

1.2 History and Evolution of Version Control Systems

The inception of version control systems (VCS) can be traced back to the early days of software development as a response to the escalating complexity and collaborative nature of programming projects. Initially, version control was managed manually, where developers would keep multiple copies of files with different naming conventions. This method quickly proved to be inefficient and error-prone, driving the need for automated tools to manage changes.

Source Code Control System (SCCS), developed by Bell Labs in the early 1970s, is often recognized as one of the first automated VCS tools. SCCS introduced the concept of tracking changes in a file over time, also known as versions or revisions. SCCS employed a diff storage model, which means it saved only the differences between file versions rather than saving the entire file each time changes were made. While SCCS was groundbreaking for its time, it had limitations, such as handling only text files and having a somewhat cumbersome interface.

Following SCCS, the **Revision Control System (RCS)**, created in the early 1980s, improved upon its predecessor by offering more user-friendly features and performance improvements. RCS continued to use delta storage techniques and expanded its capabilities to handle binary files. RCS also introduced the concept of check-in and check-out of revisions, paving the way for more organized file version tracking. The commands to manage file revisions in RCS might look like the following:

```
ci myfile.txt % Check-in a new revision
co myfile.txt % Check-out the latest revision
```

Despite the enhancements brought by RCS, it still primarily catered to individual developers, as it was not designed for highly collaborative workflows. This led to the development of systems that better supported team collaboration.

The rise of **Concurrent Versions System (CVS)** in the late 1980s marked a significant milestone in version control's evolution. CVS built upon RCS but introduced critical concepts for team collaboration, including concurrent access to repositories, branching, and merging functionalities. These advancements allowed multiple developers to work on the same project simultaneously without overwriting each other's contributions, facilitating a more seamless collaborative environment.

However, CVS had its drawbacks, including issues with atomic commits and difficulties in managing large projects with extensive branching and merging. These limitations drove the need for more sophisticated and reliable systems, leading to the introduction of **Subversion (SVN)** in the early 2000s.

SVN was designed to address and improve upon the shortcomings of CVS. It introduced the concept of atomic commits, where all changes in a commit are applied simultaneously, eliminating the risk of partial commits corrupting the repository. SVN also standardized directory versioning, which CVS lacked. Sample SVN commands are shown below:

```
svn checkout http://example.com/svn/myrepo/trunk myrepo % Check out a working
    copy
svn commit -m "Commit message" % Commit changes with a message
```

While centralized version control systems (CVCS) like CVS and SVN significantly enhanced collaborative development, they still relied on a single central repository. This reliance posed several issues, such as a single point of failure and performance bottlenecks. These limitations inspired the development of distributed version control systems (DVCS), which decentralized repository management.

Git, one of the most widely-used DVCS today, was created by Linus Torvalds in 2005. Git introduced several innovative concepts that revolutionized version control. Unlike CVCS, each developer in Git has a complete local copy of the entire repository, including all its history. This not only enhances redundancy and resilience but also allows for more flexible and efficient workflows. Git's lightweight branching and merging capabilities are highly efficient, supporting complex development patterns.

Git's architecture emphasizes speed, data integrity, and support for distributed, non-linear workflows. The following sample commands illustrate basic Git operations:

```
git clone https://github.com/example/repo.git % Clone a repository
git add . % Stage changes for commit
git commit -m "Commit message" % Commit changes with a message
git push origin main % Push commits to the remote repository
```

Around the same time, other DVCS such as **Mercurial** and **Bazaar** were also developed, offering similar functionalities to Git, but with different design philosophies and user interfaces. These tools allowed developers and organizations to choose a version control system that best matched their workflow requirements.

The development of VCS has continued to evolve with enhancements in collaboration, integration, and automation features. Modern systems often integrate closely with issue tracking, continuous integration, and deployment pipelines, providing comprehensive development ecosystems. Popular platforms like GitHub, GitLab, and Bitbucket have further expanded the utility of Git by offering additional collaboration tools, code review systems, and extensive API support.

Overall, the history and evolution of version control systems reflect the growing complexity and collaborative requirements of software development. From manual version tracking to sophisticated DVCS, these tools have become indispensable in modern development practices, supporting seamless, efficient, and reliable collaboration across diverse teams.

1.3 Types of Version Control Systems

Version control systems (VCS) can be categorized based on their architecture and the way they manage versions of files. We primarily distinguish between *local*, *centralized*, and *distributed* version control systems. Understanding these categories is critical for selecting the appropriate system tailored to specific development requirements.

Local version control systems are the simplest form of version control, wherein all the versions of a file are stored on a local disk. One common method involves creating a directory for versions within the project directory. However, this method is prone to errors since it relies heavily on manual management and organization.

More sophisticated local VCS tools, such as RCS (Revision Control System), maintain a complete history of file changes, often by keeping a set of diff files (changes between versions). This approach reduces redundancy and storage costs but still suffers from a critical limitation: it does not support collaboration among multiple users over a network.

Centralized version control systems (CVCS) were developed to address the collaboration issue inherent in local VCS. These systems, exemplified by tools like CVS (Concurrent Versions System) and Subversion (SVN), introduce a central server that stores all the versioned files. Clients check out files from the central repository, make local changes, and then check these changes back into the repository. An advantage of this model is the ease of administering a single server that holds all the history.

The centralized model also presents several inherent drawbacks:

- All users must have network access to the central repository.
- The central server represents a single point of failure; if the server

goes down, no one can collaborate or save versioned changes.

- Limited offline capabilities, as the central repository must be accessible for operations related to version management.

To counter these issues, distributed version control systems (DVCS) emerged. Tools such as Git, Mercurial, and Bazaar exemplify this category. In DVCS, every user maintains a complete local copy of the entire repository, including the full history. This paradigm offers significant benefits, including:

- Enhanced collaboration, as each user's local repository can commit changes independently without needing constant access to a central server.
- Resilience and redundancy, ensuring that no single point of failure can compromise the complete history of the project.
- Improved performance, as operations such as commits, diffs, and reverts are local and do not require network access.

Let's illustrate these characteristics with a simple example. Consider a scenario in which three developers, Alice, Bob, and Charlie, are working on a project. In a CVCS:

```
# Alice checks out the repository
$ svn checkout http://central-repo/svn/project project

# Alice makes a change
$ echo "New feature by Alice" > feature.txt
$ svn add feature.txt
$ svn commit -m "Alice's new feature"

# Bob checks out the same repository
$ svn checkout http://central-repo/svn/project project

# Bob makes changes concurrently
$ svn update # ensures Bob has the latest updates

# Bob encounters a conflict if Alice's work conflicts
$ svn resolve # Bob has to manually resolve conflicts

# Bob commits his changes
$ svn commit -m "Bob's updates"
```

Comparatively, in a DVCS like Git:

```
# Alice clones the repository
$ git clone http://central-repo.git project

# Alice makes a change
$ echo "New feature by Alice" > feature.txt
```

```
$ git add feature.txt
$ git commit -m "Alice's new feature"

# Bob clones the same repository
$ git clone http://central-repo.git project

# Bob makes changes concurrently
$ git fetch origin # updates from the central repository
$ git rebase # Integrates Alice's changes

# Bob encounters minimal conflict issues due to advanced merge capabilities
$ git commit -m "Bob's updates"
```

In the DVCS model, local operations are decoupled from the central repository. This autonomy significantly accelerates typical workflows and diminishes the dependency on constant centralized connectivity.

Both centralized and distributed systems have their own sets of advantages and limitations, but DVCS has become the dominant approach in modern development environments, notably with the widespread adoption of Git. This shift aligns with the broader trend towards decentralized and collaborative software development practices.

1.4 Centralized vs. Distributed Version Control

Version control systems (VCS) serve as critical tools in modern software development, offering structured means to manage changes over time. There exist two main categories of version control systems: centralized and distributed. Understanding the distinctions between these categories is crucial for selecting the right VCS to meet the needs of specific projects and teams.

Centralized Version Control Systems (CVCS): Centralized Version Control Systems, such as Concurrent Versions System (CVS) and Subversion (SVN), employ a client-server architecture. In this model, a single central repository serves as the authoritative source of versions. Developers perform actions such as commits, updates, and checkouts through their working copies by communicating with the central repository.

When a developer commits changes in a CVCS, those changes are immediately recorded in the central repository. This ensures that the central repository remains the definitive record of all modifications, which helps maintain consistency and integrity.

```
svn commit -m "Commit message describing changes"
```

The example command line above shows how a commit operation is conducted in Subversion (SVN). The commit includes a descriptive message that annotates the changes being submitted.

The prime advantages of CVCS are simplicity and ease of administration. As there is only one repository to manage, centralized systems can be relatively straightforward to set up and maintain. Team members can easily understand where the latest code resides, and access control can be managed comprehensively from a single point.

However, CVCS have several drawbacks:

- **Single Point of Failure:** Since all data resides on the central server, it represents a single point of failure. If the server goes down, no developer can synchronize or commit changes.
- **Limited Offline Capabilities:** Developers must have network access to work with the repository, which reduces productivity in situations where connectivity is not available.
- **Scalability Issues:** As the number of users and the size of the repository grow, performance can degrade, making operations slower.

Distributed Version Control Systems (DVCS): In contrast, Distributed Version Control Systems like Git and Mercurial use a peer-to-peer approach. Every developer's working copy comprises a complete repository, including the entire history of all changes.

This architecture allows each developer to work independently on their local repository. Commits are made locally, and any operations, such as branching or merging, can be performed without needing network access to a central server. Ultimately, developers synchronize changes with others by pushing and pulling updates between repositories.

Consider a basic scenario of committing and pushing changes in Git:

```
git commit -m "Commit message describing changes"
git push origin main
```

In this example, the first command commits the changes locally, while the second command pushes those changes to a remote repository named ‘origin‘, with the primary branch being ‘main‘.

Distributed systems offer several key benefits:

- **Robustness:** There is no single point of failure since every repository is a complete copy. Developers can continue working offline, and data loss risk is minimized.
- **Flexibility and Performance:** Operations such as branching, merging, and committing are faster because they are performed locally. This makes DVCS scalable and suitable for large projects with extensive histories.
- **Enhanced Collaboration:** By supporting multiple workflows, DVCS enables diverse collaboration models, such as feature branching and forking, which streamline parallel development.

Yet, DVCS can be more complex to administer due to the decentralized nature of the repositories. Differences in repositories can necessitate rigorous synchronization strategies, and managing access control can become intricate without a central authority.

Comparison and Use Cases: The choice between CVCS and DVCS hinges on the project's specific context and requirements. For smaller teams or projects with straightforward needs, CVCS may offer sufficient functionality with less administrative overhead. On the other hand, for larger, more distributed teams, or projects requiring robust offline capabilities and sophisticated branching models, DVCS is typically more appropriate.

Typical use cases for Centralized Version Control Systems include:

- Small to medium-sized teams with centralized operations.
- Projects where simplicity and ease of enforcement of access controls are priorities.
- Environments where network reliability is high and downtimes are minimal.

Distributed Version Control Systems are often preferred in:

- Large, geographically dispersed teams requiring high robustness.
- Projects requiring extensive branching and merging capabilities.
- Scenarios where offline work is common or necessary.

Understanding these differences enables informed decision-making when adopting a VCS, aligning the choice with the project's specific logistical and operational requirements.

1.5 Benefits of Using Version Control Systems

Version control systems (VCS) offer numerous advantages that significantly enhance the software development process. These benefits are crucial for maintaining the integrity, reliability, and efficiency of codebases as they grow and evolve. Here, we detail the primary benefits of using version control systems:

- **Collaboration and Team Coordination**
  A VCS streamlines collaboration among team members. Each developer can work on different parts of the codebase simultaneously without interfering with others' work. This is particularly essential in large teams where concurrent modifications are common. VCS provides essential mechanisms such as branching, allowing developers to isolate their changes and merge them back into the main codebase when ready. Consider the following example where two developers, Alice and Bob, work on separate features:

```
# Create a new branch for feature A
git checkout -b feature-branch-alice

# Alice makes changes and commits
git add .
git commit -m "Implemented Feature A"

# Bob creates a new branch for feature B
git checkout -b feature-branch-bob

# Bob makes changes and commits
git add .
git commit -m "Implemented Feature B"

# Merging Alice's work back to the main branch
git checkout main
git merge feature-branch-alice

# Merging Bob's work back to the main branch
git merge feature-branch-bob
```

- **Code History and Traceability**
  VCS maintains a complete history of all changes made to the

codebase. This historical record includes who made each change, when it was made, and what the change entailed. This record is indispensable for tracking the evolution of a project and for understanding why certain decisions were made. For instance, Git commands such as git log and git blame offer insights into the change history:

```
# View commit history
git log

# View line-by-line responsibility
git blame filename
```

```
Author: Alice <alice@example.com>
Date: Wed Nov 4 12:34:56 2023 -0500

    Initial commit for Feature A
```

- **Backup and Recovery**
  A VCS acts as a powerful backup tool. Since the entire history of changes is stored, it enables easy recovery from unintended modifications or deletions. Developers can revert to previous versions of the codebase should the need arise. For example, using Git, one can revert to a previous commit:

```
# Reverting to a previous commit
git revert <commit_id>
```

```
Revert "Implemented Feature A"
This reverts commit <commit_id>.
```

- **Code Integrity and Conflict Resolution**
  Using version control ensures that changes are safely integrated, maintaining code integrity. VCS systems provide robust mechanisms to detect and resolve conflicts that arise when multiple changes occur in the same portion of the codebase. This process helps ensure that merged changes do not introduce errors. During a merge conflict, Git provides a clear indication of conflict markers in the files needing resolution:

```
<<<<<<< HEAD
Current changes in the main branch
=======
Incoming changes from the feature branch
>>>>>>> feature-branch
```

- **Branching and Experimentation**
  Branching, a core feature in VCS, facilitates experimenting with new features without affecting the mainline code. Developers can create branches to test new features, bug fixes, or refactorings, ensuring the main branch remains stable. If the experiment is

successful, it is merged into the main branch; otherwise, it can be discarded without repercussions.

```
# Create a new feature branch
git checkout -b experimental-feature

# If successful, merge back to the main branch
git checkout main
git merge experimental-feature

# Delete the experimental branch
git branch -d experimental-feature
```

- **Audit and Compliance**
  VCS facilitates auditing and compliance by providing immutable records of code changes. This is particularly important in industries with stringent regulatory requirements. Complete records aid in demonstrating adherence to standards and processes during audits.

- **Enhanced Code Review Process**
  Version control systems streamline the code review process. Changes can be easily reviewed and commented on before being integrated, ensuring code quality and adherence to best practices. Using pull requests, a common feature in modern VCS like Git, developers can propose changes and request reviews from peers:

```
# Push changes to remote repository
git push origin feature-branch

# Open a pull request from the feature branch to the main branch
# Reviewers can comment and approve the changes
```

- **Distributed Development Capability**
  Distributed VCS like Git allow for a distributed development model where each team member has a complete copy of the repository, including its full history. This decentralization enhances collaboration and allows for greater flexibility and resilience, as work can continue even when remote access to a central server is not possible.

Each of these benefits shows the indispensability of VCS in modern software development practices, facilitating efficient collaboration, preserving code integrity, and enabling traceability and auditing.

1.6 Key Concepts and Terminology

Understanding the core concepts and terminology used in version control systems is crucial for effectively managing and collaborating on software projects. In this section, we will explore these concepts and terms, providing clear and precise definitions to ensure a solid foundational knowledge that will facilitate the use of version control systems like Git.

Repository (Repo): A repository, often referred to simply as a "repo," is the central location where all the files and versions of a project are stored. It functions as a comprehensive database that tracks all changes made to the files within the project over time.

Commit: A commit represents a snapshot of the project's files at a specific point in time. Each commit is uniquely identified by a hash, typically generated using a cryptographic function like SHA-1. Commits allow developers to capture changes made to the codebase, making it possible to revert to previous states if necessary. A commit message, which describes the changes made, should accompany each commit for clarity and context.

```
$ git add .
$ git commit -m "Fixed bug in user authentication module"
```

Branch: A branch in a version control system is a parallel version of the repository. Branches allow developers to work on different features, bug fixes, or experiments simultaneously without affecting the main codebase. The primary branch in most Git repositories is called "main" or "master."

Merge: Merging is the process of integrating changes from one branch into another. This operation combines the distinct changes made in different branches to create a unified history. When conflicts arise during a merge, they must be resolved manually by the developer.

```
$ git checkout main
$ git merge feature-branch
```

Clone: Cloning is the act of creating a local copy of a remote repository. This operation is fundamental for collaboration, enabling multiple developers to work on the same project from different locations.

```
$ git clone https://github.com/user/repo.git
```

Pull: The pull operation is used to fetch and integrate changes from a remote repository into the current branch of a local repository. It is a combination of "fetch" and "merge" operations.

```
$ git pull origin main
```

Push: Pushing involves sending the committed changes from a local repository to a remote repository. This operation updates the remote repository with the latest changes from the local repository.

```
$ git push origin main
```

Fork: Forking is the process of creating a personal copy of someone else's repository on a hosting service like GitHub. This allows developers to freely experiment with changes without affecting the original repository.

Remote: A remote, in Git terminology, refers to a common repository that all team members use for exchanging changes. "origin" is the default name given to the remote repository.

```
$ git remote add origin https://github.com/user/repo.git
```

Rebase: Rebasing is an alternative to merging. It allows for the integration of changes from one branch onto another by moving or applying commits to a new base. This operation can produce a cleaner project history, as it avoids the additional merge commits.

```
$ git checkout feature-branch
$ git rebase main
```

Conflict: A conflict occurs when two or more commits from different branches modify the same part of a file, resulting in incompatible changes. Conflicts must be resolved manually by the developer during the merge or rebase process.

```
Conflict:
<<<<<<< HEAD
// changes in current branch
=======
// changes in incoming branch
>>>>>>> incoming-branch
```

Tag: Tags are named references to specific commits, often used to mark release points (e.g., version 1.0, 2.0). Tags provide a convenient way of tracking versions and stable points in the project's history.

```
$ git tag -a v1.0 -m "Release version 1.0"
$ git push origin v1.0
```

Stash: Stashing allows developers to temporarily save changes in their working directory without committing them. This is useful when switching contexts, such as moving between different branches without losing work in progress.

```
$ git stash
$ git stash apply
```

Each of these concepts plays a critical role in the everyday workflow of version control, especially in distributed systems like Git. Understanding and effectively utilizing these elements not only aids in managing a codebase but also fosters better collaboration and more efficient development practices.

1.7 Common Use Cases and Scenarios

Version control systems (VCS) are indispensable in modern software development, providing robust mechanisms for tracking changes, fostering collaboration, and maintaining the integrity of codebases. The applications of VCS extend far beyond a single use case, encapsulating a wide array of scenarios where its functionality proves to be essential. This section elaborates on various common use cases and scenarios where version control systems play a pivotal role.

One of the primary use cases of VCS is in collaborative software development. When multiple developers work on the same project, coordination becomes critical. Version control provides a structured environment where each developer can work on different aspects of the project simultaneously. Changes made by individual developers are tracked, and their contributions are merged systematically into the shared repository. This process avoids conflicts and ensures consistency.

```
git clone https://github.com/example/repo.git
```

Upon cloning the repository, each developer can create branches to work on specific features or bug fixes without interfering with the main codebase.

```
git checkout -b feature/new-feature
```

Another significant use case is maintaining a history of changes. Version control systems maintain a detailed record of every change made to the codebase, including what was changed, who made the changes, and when the changes were made. This historical context is invaluable, especially when debugging an issue. If a bug is introduced, developers can trace back through the commit history to identify when and why a change was made, facilitating more efficient debugging and regression testing.

```
git log
```

In open-source projects, version control systems enable external contributors to contribute to the project with ease. Contributors can fork the repository, make their changes, and submit pull requests for review.

```
# Fork the repository via GitHub interface and clone your fork:
git clone https://github.com/username/repo.git
```

The project maintainers can review these pull requests, provide feedback, and merge the changes if they meet the project's standards.

```
git push origin feature/new-feature
```

In academic settings, version control systems are increasingly being used for managing and tracking changes in research projects, especially those that involve collaborative coding or writing. Whether it's for tracking the development of new algorithms, maintaining datasets, or managing document revisions, VCS provides a transparent and reproducible way to document the evolution of research work.

```
git add <file>
git commit -m "Added new dataset"
```

Version control systems also facilitate code reviews and quality control. Through features like pull requests and code comments, teams can enforce coding standards and ensure code quality before integrating changes into the main branch. This peer-review process helps catch potential issues early and promotes knowledge sharing among team members.

```
# Navigate to the pull requests section on GitHub, review changes, and comment:
git checkout -b review/feature/new-feature
```

Integrating VCS with automated build and deployment systems can significantly enhance the productivity of development teams. Continuous Integration (CI) and Continuous Deployment (CD) pipelines are often configured to trigger builds and tests automatically upon each commit, ensuring that the new changes do not break the established functionality. This automation helps maintain a stable development environment and accelerates the delivery process.

```
all: build test
```

```
build:
    @echo "Building the project..."
    # Build commands here

test:
    @echo "Running tests..."
    # Test commands here
```

The ability to branch and merge is another critical use case for VCS, supporting various development methodologies like GitFlow, feature branching, and trunk-based development. Branching allows developers to experiment and develop new features or hotfixes independently of the main codebase.

```
git checkout main
git merge feature/new-feature
```

Version control systems are also indispensable in managing configuration files and scripts across different environments. Keeping environment-specific configurations in separate branches or leveraging environment variables helps maintain consistency and simplify deployments.

```
export DB_HOST="localhost"
export DB_USER="user"
export DB_PASS="password"
```

Finally, version control systems provide a safety net through their ability to roll back to previous states of the codebase. If a critical issue is discovered, the team can revert to a stable version, minimizing downtime and reducing the risk of significant disruptions.

```
git revert <commit-hash>
```

These examples illustrate the versatility and robustness of version control systems in different scenarios, underlining their importance in modern software development and beyond.

Chapter 2

Getting Started with Git

This chapter provides a foundational understanding of Git, starting with an introduction to its purpose and significance in version control. It guides you through the installation process and initial setup of a Git repository. Key topics include configuring Git for the first time, understanding the structure and significance of the .git directory, and making your initial commit. The chapter also covers cloning existing repositories and introduces various Git GUI tools and Integrated Development Environments (IDEs) to facilitate a seamless development experience.

2.1 Introduction to Git

Git is a distributed version control system that enables individuals and teams to manage changes to source code over time. Unlike centralized version control systems such as Subversion and CVS, Git allows for a complete copy of the entire repository, including its full history, on each developer's machine. This architecture provides several benefits, including better performance and the ability to manage code in a decentralized manner.

From a technical standpoint, Git tracks changes using a combination of snapshots and a directed acyclic graph (DAG). Each time you commit changes, Git captures a snapshot of your files and stores a reference to that snapshot. This snapshot contains metadata, including a unique SHA-1 hash, timestamps, and references to its parent commits. As subsequent commits are made, Git links these snapshots together, forming a chain that represents the project's history.

Below is an example illustrating the SHA-1 hash generation for a simple text object using Git's internal hashing mechanism:

```
echo "Hello Git" | git hash-object --stdin
# Output: 8ab686eafeb1a5f4f3e18725aba02eb316f7b0f0
```

This command pipes the string "Hello Git" into the git hash-object command, which then generates the SHA-1 hash, representing the content's unique identifier in the repository.

Key concepts in Git include repositories, branches, commits, and merges. A Git repository (repo) is a data structure that stores metadata for a set of files and directories. This metadata includes information about file changes over time and is organized into branches. Branches are pointers to specific commits, allowing you to work on different aspects of your project simultaneously. The default branch in a new Git repository is typically named main, though older repositories might use master.

A commit is a record of changes, and each commit has a unique identifier generated using SHA-1 hashing. A commit also includes metadata like the author, timestamp, and commit message. The relationship between commits forms the repository's history, enabling you to track changes and revert to previous states if necessary.

A merge operation integrates changes from different branches. When merging, Git attempts to reconcile differences between the branches, resulting in either an automatic merge or a conflict. A conflict occurs when changes from different branches cannot be automatically reconciled. Below is a basic example illustrating the creation of a repository, making initial commits, and performing a merge:

```
# Initialize a new repository
git init my_repo
cd my_repo

# Create a file and commit it
echo "First line" > file.txt
git add file.txt
git commit -m "Initial commit"

# Create a new branch and make a commit
git checkout -b new-branch
echo "Second line" >> file.txt
git add file.txt
git commit -m "Add second line in new-branch"

# Switch back to main branch and merge
```

```
git checkout main
echo "Third line" >> file.txt
git add file.txt
git commit -m "Add third line in main branch"

# Perform the merge
git merge new-branch
```

If the changes on the different branches do not interfere with each other, the merge completes automatically. Otherwise, Git produces a conflict and presents it in the files, which need resolution manually before completing the merge.

To understand Git's role in modern software development, it's crucial to recognize the collaborative nature of programming. Collaborative development requires coordination and a mechanism to manage changes from multiple contributors. Git's distributed model facilitates this by allowing each developer to work independently while maintaining the ability to synchronize their changes with others. Through commands such as git pull, git push, and git fetch, developers can exchange changes between repositories, ensuring a coherent project evolution.

Below is a representation of common Git commands and their purposes:

- **Command** and **Description**:

git init	Initializes a new Git repository
git clone <url>	Clones an existing repository from a specified URL
git status	Displays the state of the working directory and staging area
git add <file>	Stages changes for the next commit
git commit -m "message"	Records changes to the repository with a message
git push	Uploads local repository content to a remote repository
git pull	Fetches and integrates changes from a remote repository to the current branch
git merge <branch>	Merges the specified branch's history into the current branch
git branch	Lists branches, optionally also creates or deletes them

Understanding these basic commands enables effective interaction with Git. Repositories can be synchronized with remote servers (e.g., GitHub, GitLab, Bitbucket) to facilitate collaboration across diverse geographical locations.

Git has become an essential tool in the software development ecosystem. Its distributed nature ensures robust collaboration, fault tolerance, and efficient version management across projects of varying complexity and scale. Whether working on small personal projects or large enterprise applications, mastering Git's fundamentals is crucial for modern software development.

2.2 Installing Git

To harness the capabilities of Git, the first step is to install it on your machine. The installation process varies based on the operating system you are using – Windows, macOS, or Linux. In this section, we provide detailed instructions for each of these operating systems to ensure a smooth installation process.

1. **Installing Git on Windows**

   For Windows users, the recommended way to install Git is by using the Git for Windows package, which includes Git Bash, a command-line interface that emulates a Unix shell, supporting most of the standard Unix commands.

   (a) Navigate to the official Git website: https://git-scm.com/

   (b) Click on the *Download* button. This will automatically detect your operating system and provide the appropriate Git for Windows installer.

   (c) Once the download is complete, run the installer executable file (e.g., Git-2.x.x-64-bit.exe).

   (d) Follow the installation wizard, which includes several steps:

   - **Select Destination Location:** Choose the directory where Git will be installed. By default, it is usually C:\Program Files\Git.
   - **Select Components:** Opt to include the Git Bash and Git GUI, as well as integration with the Windows Explorer context menu.
   - **Adjusting Your PATH Environment:** Choose either to use Git from the command line and also from 3rd-party software (recommended for beginners) or from Git Bash only. The first option adds Git to your system PATH.
   - **Choosing the SSH executable:** Use the OpenSSH bundled with Git is often preferable for most users.

- **Choosing SSL/TLS Library:** OpenSSL is a standard choice.
- **Configuring Line Ending Conversions:** Select Checkout Windows-style, commit Unix-style line endings.
- **Configuring the terminal emulator:** Choose Use MinTTY (the default terminal of Git Bash).
- **Additional Options:** Enable file system caching and other performance optimizations provided by Git for Windows.

(e) Complete the installation process and launch Git Bash to verify the installation.

To confirm that Git has been installed correctly, open Git Bash and enter the command:

```
git --version
```

The output should be similar to:

```
git version 2.x.x
```

2. **Installing Git on macOS**

macOS users can install Git via several methods, including the official binary installer, Homebrew, or Xcode Command Line Tools. Here, we detail the Homebrew installation process as it simplifies version management.

(a) If Homebrew is not already installed on your system, you can install it by running the following command in the Terminal:

```
/bin/bash -c "$(curl -fsSL https://raw.githubusercontent.com/
    Homebrew/install/HEAD/install.sh)"
```

(b) Once Homebrew is installed, update it to ensure you have the latest package definitions:

```
brew update
```

(c) Now, install Git using Homebrew:

```
brew install git
```

(d) To confirm that Git has been installed successfully, check the version:

```
git --version
```

The output should reflect the installed Git version, e.g.,

```
git version 2.x.x
```

3. **Installing Git on Linux**

   For Linux distributions, Git can be installed using the package manager associated with your specific distribution. Below are the commands for some popular distributions:

   - **Debian-based distributions (Ubuntu, Linux Mint):**

     ```
     sudo apt update
     sudo apt install git
     ```

   - **Red Hat-based distributions (Fedora, CentOS):**

     ```
     sudo dnf install git
     ```

   - **Arch-based distributions:**

     ```
     sudo pacman -S git
     ```

   To verify the installation, run the following command in your terminal:

   ```
   git --version
   ```

   The output should indicate the installed Git version:

   ```
   git version 2.x.x
   ```

2.3 Setting Up Your First Repository

Establishing your first Git repository is a critical step towards effective version control and collaborative software development. The process involves the creation of a new repository, initializing it, and making your initial configurations. This section will provide a comprehensive guide to setting up your first repository.

To begin with, navigate to the directory where you want to create your project. Open your terminal (or command line interface) and execute the following command to create a new directory for your project:

```
mkdir my_first_project
```

The mkdir command is used here to create a new directory named my_first_project. Next, move into this newly created directory using the cd command:

```
cd my_first_project
```

Once you are within your project directory, you can initialize a new Git repository by executing the following command:

```
git init
```

The git init command transforms the current directory into a Git repository. This command creates a hidden directory named .git which contains all the metadata and object database for the project. To confirm that your directory is now a Git repository, you can list the contents of the directory and ensure the presence of the .git folder:

```
ls -a
```

You should see an output similar to:

```
. .. .git
```

Next, let's create a simple file and add it to the repository. For this example, we will create a README.md file. You can use any text editor to create the file. For simplicity, you can also use the echo command:

```
echo "# My First Git Project" > README.md
```

This command creates a file named README.md and writes the text # My First Git Project into it. To add this file to the staging area, use the following command:

```
git add README.md
```

The git add command adds the specified files to the staging area, preparing them to be included in the next commit. To commit the staged changes, execute the following command:

```
git commit -m "Initial commit"
```

The git commit command records the changes in the repository, capturing the current state of the project at that point in time. The -m flag allows you to include a commit message directly from the command line; in this case, the message is "Initial commit."

You can now view the commit history using the git log command:

```
git log
```

The output should be similar to the following:

```
commit e68f14d89ba6f84bced50ae32141707e632a23e0
Author: Your Name <youremail@example.com>
Date:   Wed Mar 15 13:58:10 2023 +0100

    Initial commit
```

At this stage, your repository contains a single commit that includes the README.md file. Git tracks the changes in the repository from this initial commit forward.

To verify the current status of your repository, use the git status command:

```
git status
```

This command provides information about the state of the working directory and staging area. For a clean state, you should see a message indicating that there are no changes to be committed.

Another useful command at this point is git diff, which shows the changes that have been made but are not yet staged. Since no modifications were made after the initial commit, the current output would be empty.

At this juncture, your Git repository is properly set up and ready for further development. As new files are created or existing files are modified, you'll need to add and commit those changes using the commands outlined above.

Should you wish to include your repository on a remote server, such as GitHub, you would initialize the remote configuration with the following commands:

```
git remote add origin https://github.com/yourusername/my_first_project.git
git push -u origin master
```

Here, git remote add origin associates the local repository with a remote repository. Thereafter, git push -u origin master pushes the committed files to the remote repository and sets up the upstream tracking for the master branch.

This setup forms the foundation for more advanced features and workflows in Git, including branching and merging, which will be covered in subsequent chapters.

2.4 Basic Git Configuration

Once Git has been successfully installed on your system, the next crucial step involves configuring it appropriately to streamline your workflow. The configuration process in Git is straightforward but highly customizable, allowing you to tailor the tool to suit your specific needs. We will focus on setting up your identity, configuring default behaviors, and understanding Git's configuration hierarchy.

To begin configuring Git, the primary command you will employ is git config. This command enables you to alter settings at various levels, including local, global, and system-wide configurations. Let's delve into each of these configurations in detail.

1. Setting Your Identity

The first step in configuring Git is to set your identity. This is essential because Git attaches your name and email address to each commit you make, thus ensuring that your contributions are correctly attributed. This configuration can be done globally (affecting all repositories) or locally (on a per-repository basis). To set your global username and email address, use the following commands:

```
git config --global user.name "Your Name"
git config --global user.email "your.email@example.com"
```

If you prefer to set your identity for a specific repository only, navigate to that repository and omit the -global flag:

```
git config user.name "Your Name"
git config user.email "your.email@example.com"
```

2. Configuring Default Text Editor

Git frequently requires you to input messages, especially for commit and merge operations. By default, Git uses the system's default text editor, which might not be to your preference. You can specify a text editor by setting the core.editor property. For instance, to set Visual Studio Code as the default editor, use:

```
git config --global core.editor "code --wait"
```

For Vim users, the command would be:

```
git config --global core.editor "vim"
```

3. Configuring Line Endings

Managing line endings is crucial, especially in environments where multiple operating systems are involved. Git can automatically handle line ending conversions. To configure Git for this task, employ the following commands:

For Windows users working in a mixed OS environment:

```
git config --global core.autocrlf true
```

For macOS and Linux users:

```
git config --global core.autocrlf input
```

4. Aliases

Creating aliases for frequently used Git commands can significantly improve productivity. Aliases are shortcuts that reference longer commands. For example, to create an alias for `git status`, use:

```
git config --global alias.st status
```

Now, you can use `git st` instead of `git status`. Another useful alias might be:

```
git config --global alias.co checkout
```

5. Viewing Configuration

To review the configuration settings you have applied, use the command:

```
git config --list
```

This will display all current configurations, spanning user credentials, editor settings, and aliases.

6. Git Configuration Levels

Understanding the hierarchy of Git configuration is essential:

- **Local Configuration:** Applies only to a specific repository. Use the `git config` command without the `–global` or `–system` flag.
- **Global Configuration:** Applies to the user account on the system. Commands containing the `–global` flag affect this level.
- **System Configuration:** Applies to all users on the system. Use the `–system` flag to read or write configurations at this level.

To specify a configuration level explicitly, precede the command with the appropriate flag. For instance, setting the default merge tool at the global level would be:

```
git config --global merge.tool vimdiff
```

To remove a configuration, the –unset flag can be used:

```
git config --global --unset user.name
git config --global --unset user.email
```

The depth and flexibility of Git's configuration options allow tailored setups for various workflows and environments. Proper configuration lays the foundation for effective version control management.

2.5 Understanding the .git Directory

The .git directory is a critical component of a Git repository. When you initialize a new repository with the git init command, Git creates the .git directory to store all version-controlled data. This hidden directory houses the repository's metadata and essential configuration files, making it the brain of your Git project. A thorough understanding of the .git directory is fundamental to mastering Git.

Structure of the .git Directory

```
.git/
 HEAD
 config
 description
 hooks/
 info/
 objects/
 refs/
 logs/
    HEAD
    refs/
 index
```

HEAD is a crucial file that represents the current branch's tip. This file contains a reference to the most recent commit on the currently checked-out branch. For instance, if you are working on the main branch, the HEAD file might contain:

```
ref: refs/heads/main
```

The config file stores repository-specific configuration settings. These settings override the global configurations typically stored in the

~/.gitconfig file. The format of the config file is similar to the following:

```
[core]
    repositoryformatversion = 0
    filemode = true
    bare = false
[remote "origin"]
    url = https://github.com/user/repo.git
    fetch = +refs/heads/*:refs/remotes/origin/*
```

The description file is mainly used by Git web interfaces to describe the repository. For most standard uses, this file can stay as its default text.

The hooks directory contains client-side and server-side scripts that Git will execute in response to certain events. Examples include pre-commit, prepare-commit-msg, post-commit, and others. These hooks can be used to enforce policies or to trigger actions at specified points.

The info directory contains two files, exclude and attributes, that provide repository-specific information on ignored files and custom file attributes respectively. The exclude file allows users to specify the paths to ignore specific files or directories within the repository, similar to the .gitignore file.

The objects directory holds all the objects that make up the repository's history. This includes commits, trees, and blobs, all stored under unique SHA-1 hashes. The structure is divided into 256 subdirectories (01-ff), facilitating quick access:

```
objects/
 17/
    eb2c8e1cff840c6f07d355c6ef79e3bc2dbe9b
 3d/
    cfd8a77797d7b6167faa9964eccdfaea1c8b...
 pack/
    pack-e3b0c44298fc1c149afbf4c8996f092d...
    pack-e3b0c44298fc1c149afbf4c8996f092d...
```

The refs directory contains references to objects stored in the repository, classified into heads, remotes, and tags. Reference heads typically point to the latest commit of a branch, stored in:

```
refs/
 heads/
    main
 remotes/
   origin/
      main
 tags/
    v1.0
```

The logs directory maintains records of all reference updates, aiding in the debugging and review of repository history. For instance, the logs/HEAD file logs changes made to the HEAD reference:

```
logs/
 HEAD
 refs/
     heads/
         main
     remotes/
         origin/
             main
```

index is a binary file representing the current staging area. It captures the state of the working directory in preparation for the next commit. The index file ensures coherence between the working directory and the repository.

By parsing the intricacies of each component within the .git directory, users gain comprehensive insight into how Git operates behind the scenes. This knowledge enhances adeptness in utilizing Git for version control, troubleshooting issues, and tailoring Git to specific needs.

2.6 Initial Commit and History

After successfully setting up your Git repository and configuring basic settings, the next fundamental step is to make your initial commit. This initial commit establishes the first snapshot of the files in your project directory. It marks a significant milestone, representing the baseline state of your code. Once committed, Git will begin tracking changes to these files, thereby allowing you to manage and navigate through your project's evolution.

To make an initial commit, ensure your project directory contains files you wish to track. You can create or copy files into this directory as necessary. Navigate to the root of your project directory using the terminal or command prompt. Git operations within the repository should always be executed from its root directory or its subdirectories.

First, you need to add the files to the staging area. The staging area, also known as the index, is an intermediate area where Git tracks changes to be committed. Adding files to the staging area involves using the git add command followed by the file name or a pattern.

```
git add .
```

The git add . command stages all files and directories in the current directory. It is crucial to replace the period (.) with specific file names or patterns if you do not intend to stage all changes. For example:

```
git add README.md src/
```

This command stages the README.md file and all files within the src/ directory. Before committing, review the status of your repository to ensure that the intended changes are staged. Execute the following command:

```
git status
```

The output indicates which files are staged for commit. For instance:

```
On branch master

No commits yet

Changes to be committed:
  (use "git rm --cached <file>..." to unstage)
        new file:   README.md
        new file:   src/main.py
```

This status message confirms that the README.md and src/main.py files are staged for commit. To finalize the initial commit, use the git commit command. This command records the changes in the local repository, creating a new commit object.

```
git commit -m "Initial commit"
```

The -m option allows you to include a commit message directly from the command line. It is a best practice to write descriptive commit messages that accurately convey the purpose and scope of the changes. The example above uses "Initial commit" to describe this first submission.

Once committed, you can view the history of the repository using the git log command. The git log provides a detailed chronological record of commits.

```
git log
```

A typical output of the git log command might look like the following:

```
commit d1e8d92a2a4b6b5e4d8f3e0ba8ec0b7a6a06d68d (HEAD -> master)
Author: Your Name <your.email@example.com>
Date:   Tue Mar 28 11:45:00 2023 -0700

    Initial commit
```

This output includes the commit hash, author information, date, and the commit message. The commit hash (e.g., d1e8d92a2a4b6b5e4d8f3e0ba8ec0b7a6a06d68d) uniquely identifies the commit. The HEAD label indicates the current position in the commit history, pointing to the latest commit in the active branch. In this case, HEAD points to the "master" branch.

Understanding commit history is crucial for tracking project evolution, diagnosing issues, and collaborating with others. Each commit acts as a point-in-time snapshot of the repository, enabling you to revert to previous states if necessary.

To summarize, making an initial commit involves staging files with git add , committing them with git commit -m, and reviewing the commit history with git log. By following these steps, you establish a solid foundation for managing changes to your project and leveraging the powerful capabilities of Git's version control system.

2.7 Cloning an Existing Repository

Cloning an existing repository is a fundamental operation in Git that allows you to create a local copy of a remote repository. This action is essential not only for collaboration but also for backup purposes and offline development. When you clone a repository, Git creates a directory on your local machine that contains all files and history from the remote repository. This section will walk you through the process of cloning a repository, detailing each step to ensure clarity and understanding.

The command used to clone a repository in Git is git clone. The basic syntax for this command is as follows:

```
git clone <repository_url>
```

Here, <repository_url> is the URL of the remote repository you wish to clone. The git clone command supports various protocols, including HTTPS, SSH, and GIT.

Understanding the cloning process involves several operations that Git performs behind the scenes:

- Git initializes a new repository in a directory named after the repository unless a different directory name is specified.
- It fetches all the data from the remote repository, including branches, tags, and the entire commit history.

- Git automatically checks out the latest version of the default branch (usually main or master).

For instance, to clone a repository hosted on GitHub, the command would be:

```
git clone https://github.com/username/repository.git
```

If you prefer to use SSH for enhanced security, the command changes slightly:

```
git clone git@github.com:username/repository.git
```

By default, the repository will be cloned into a directory with the same name as the repository. However, you can specify a different directory name by adding it to the end of the git clone command:

```
git clone https://github.com/username/repository.git custom-directory-name
```

This command will clone the contents of repository.git into a directory named custom-directory-name.

By default, Git clones the default branch of the repository. To clone a different branch, use the -b option followed by the branch name:

```
git clone -b branch-name https://github.com/username/repository.git
```

For example, to clone the branch named development, you would use:

```
git clone -b development https://github.com/username/repository.git
```

Cloning an entire repository can sometimes be overkill, especially if you are only interested in the latest changes. To clone a repository with a limited number of commits, use the –depth option:

```
git clone --depth 1 https://github.com/username/repository.git
```

The –depth 1 option creates a shallow copy with only the most recent commit, reducing the time and storage required for the clone.

After cloning a repository, navigate into the newly created directory using the cd command:

```
cd repository
```

You now have access to the complete history of the repository and can begin making changes. It is good practice to examine the branches and tags available in the cloned repository:

```
git branch -a
```

```
git tag -l
```

These commands provide an overview of the repository's structure and help you understand its current state.

Cloning a repository is not just a means of obtaining code but encompasses gaining access to the entire history and collaborative efforts of a project. Ensuring that you understand the various options and their implications enhances your ability to effectively manage and contribute to Git repositories. Every clone operation is a foundational step toward efficient and reliable version control.

2.8 Exploring the Git GUI Tools

Git, primarily accessed through the command line, also offers a variety of graphical user interfaces (GUIs) to facilitate the version control process. These tools provide a more visual and intuitive way to interact with Git repositories, making them especially useful for those who prefer visual over textual interaction or those who are new to Git.

Git GUI Tools Overview: Several Git GUI tools exist, each with unique features and interfaces suited to different workflows and preferences. Commonly used Git GUI tools include GitKraken, Sourcetree, GitHub Desktop, and TortoiseGit.

GitKraken: GitKraken is known for its user-friendly interface and comprehensive features that cater to both individuals and teams. It offers a unified view of the entire repository, including branches, commits, and file changes, which helps in understanding the repository's history and current state. GitKraken also supports GitFlow and integrates with various services like GitHub, GitLab, and Bitbucket.

```
# Example of GitFlow initialization in GitKraken
git flow init
```

Sourcetree: Sourcetree is another powerful Git GUI tool that provides full-featured visual management of repositories. It simplifies complicated Git commands into a visual interface, making it easier for users to track changes, branch histories, and manage conflicts. Sourcetree offers comprehensive diff and merge tools, which are crucial for resolving merge conflicts efficiently.

```
# Example clone repository command in Sourcetree
git clone https://github.com/user/repo.git
```

GitHub Desktop: GitHub Desktop is a simple yet effective Git GUI client developed by GitHub. It seamlessly integrates with GitHub repositories and offers features like pull requests, issues, and team collaboration tools directly within the application. Users can easily create, branch, commit, push, and pull directly from the GUI, making it a great tool for GitHub users.

```
# Example of creating a new branch in GitHub Desktop
git checkout -b new-branch
```

TortoiseGit: TortoiseGit extends the functionality of Git by integrating with the Windows Shell, allowing users to manage repositories directly through Windows Explorer. It is highly customizable, with a variety of options for diffing and merging. TortoiseGit also provides extensive logging and visualization tools to better understand repository changes over time.

```
# Example of committing changes in TortoiseGit
git commit -m "message"
```

Key Features and Usability: While each GUI tool has unique features, they generally share common functionalities that enhance usability:

- **Visual Commit History:** Graphical tools display commit histories in a straightforward, visual format, making it easier to track changes and navigate between commits.
- **Branch Management:** Most Git GUIs provide a visual representation of branches, allowing users to create, merge, and delete branches with ease.
- **Conflict Resolution:** Diff and merge tools in GUI applications simplify the process of resolving merge conflicts by providing side-by-side comparisons of changes.
- **Integrated Workflows:** Direct integration with popular platforms like GitHub, GitLab, and Bitbucket streamlines the workflow by providing quick access to issues, pull requests, and other repository-related activities.

Configuring and Using Git GUI Tools: To start using a Git GUI tool, download and install the software from the official website. Once installed, configuration involves connecting the GUI tool to your repository and setting up user preferences. For example, to configure GitKraken, you might need to sign in with your GitHub or GitLab account and clone your repository.

Example Configuration Process for GitKraken:

```
# 1. Open GitKraken and sign in using your preferred Git service.
# 2. Click on the "Clone a repo" option.
# 3. Enter the repository URL and select the destination folder.
# 4. Click on "Clone the repo" to complete the process.
```

Exploring Essential Functions: Once configured, exploring the graphical interface and understanding its essential functions is crucial. Features such as staging changes, committing, pushing, and pulling can be executed through buttons and menus.

Example Actions in GitHub Desktop:

```
# To stage changes:
# 1. Modify files in your repository as needed.
# 2. GitHub Desktop will automatically detect changes.
# 3. Under "Changes" tab, select the files to stage and click on "Commit to <branch-
     name>".

# To push changes:
# 1. Once changes are committed, click on "Push origin" to update the remote
     repository.
```

Using these Git GUI tools, users can effectively manage their repositories without needing advanced Git command line proficiency. Each tool's visual and interactive elements make the operations more intuitive, aiding both new and experienced users.

2.9 Using Git with Integrated Development Environments (IDEs)

Integrated Development Environments (IDEs) significantly simplify the workflow for developers by providing a unified interface that incorporates various tools, including version control systems like Git. Many popular IDEs offer built-in support for Git, which can streamline the process of managing source code changes directly within the development environment. This section explores how to integrate Git with some of the leading IDEs, focusing on the setup process, common tasks, and key features available.

Connecting Git with Visual Studio Code (VS Code)

Visual Studio Code (VS Code) is a versatile and highly extensible code editor developed by Microsoft. It offers robust Git integration that allows for seamless version control operations directly within the editor.

Step 1: Installing the Git Extension

Ensure Git is installed on your system. Verify the installation by running:

```
git --version
```

Once Git is installed, open VS Code. If the Git extension is not already enabled, navigate to the Extensions view by clicking the Extensions icon in the Activity Bar on the side of the window or pressing Ctrl+Shift+X. Search for "Git" and install the Git extension provided by VS Code.

Step 2: Initializing a Repository

To initialize a new Git repository, open the VS Code command palette using Ctrl+Shift+P and select Git: Initialize Repository. You will be prompted to choose a directory to initialize as the repository. Select the desired folder and VS Code will set it up as a Git repository.

Step 3: Performing Git Operations

VS Code provides an intuitive interface for Git operations. Common actions such as committing changes, creating branches, and pushing or pulling from remote repositories can be performed using the Source Control view.

- *Committing Changes:* In the Source Control view, modified files are displayed. To commit changes, stage the files by clicking the plus icon next to them, write a commit message in the message box, and click the checkmark to commit.
- *Creating Branches:* Use the branch icon on the lower left of the window to create or switch branches. You can view branches, create new ones, and switch between them using the interface.
- *Pushing and Pulling:* Use the menu options available in the Source Control view to push commits to a remote repository or pull updates.

Using Git with PyCharm

PyCharm, developed by JetBrains, is another prominent IDE, especially beneficial for Python developers. PyCharm includes integrated

Git support, offering a comprehensive interface for source control operations.

Step 1: Configuring Git in PyCharm

After installing Git on your system, configure PyCharm to recognize Git:

1. Open PyCharm and navigate to File > Settings > Version Control > Git.
2. Ensure the path to the Git executable is correct. Click Test to verify the configuration.

Step 2: Cloning a Repository

To clone a repository, go to File > New > Project from Version Control > Git. Enter the repository URL and choose the destination directory. PyCharm will clone the repository and open it in the IDE.

Step 3: Git Operations in PyCharm

In PyCharm, version control operations can be performed via the VCS menu or the Version Control tool window:

- *Committing Changes:* Access the Commit window using Ctrl+K. Stage changes, write a commit message, and commit the changes.
- *Branch Management:* Use the Git branch widget at the bottom right corner of the IDE. This provides options for creating, renaming, merging, and deleting branches.
- *Push and Pull:* Use the dedicated icons or the VCS menu to push your commits to the remote repository or pull updates.

Integration with Other IDEs

Apart from VS Code and PyCharm, many other IDEs such as IntelliJ IDEA, Eclipse, and NetBeans offer built-in Git support or plugins that can be installed to provide Git functionality. Generally, these integrations offer similar features:

Initial Setup:

Most IDEs require an initial configuration where you specify the path to your Git executable. This can usually be done in the settings/preferences menu under the version control or Git section.

Cloning Repositories:

IDEs often offer a straightforward interface to clone repositories. This usually involves providing the repository URL and choosing a local directory.

Common Operations:

Frequent Git operations like committing changes, creating and merging branches, fetching updates, and pushing commits are typically integrated into the IDE's menu system or accessible through dedicated tool windows and panels. This integration ensures that developers can make use of Git functionality without leaving their development environment, increasing productivity and maintaining focus on coding tasks.

Understanding how to leverage Git within your IDE of choice helps streamline version control, contributing to a more efficient and organized development process. The deep integration of version control features within IDEs ensures ease of access to essential Git operations, fostering a collaborative and well-managed coding environment.

Chapter 3

Basic Git Operations

This chapter delves into fundamental Git operations, explaining how to manage the working directory, staging area, and repository. It covers essential commands for committing changes, viewing commit history, and creating Git ignore files. The chapter also addresses staging and unstaging changes, inspecting differences with Git diff, and handling operations like reverting, deleting, renaming, and moving files. Additionally, it introduces the effective use of Git log for tracking project history.

3.1 Understanding the Working Directory, Staging Area, and Repository

In Git, the structure of the version control environment is fundamental to understanding how changes are tracked and managed. Git organizes files into three major areas: the Working Directory, the Staging Area, and the Repository. Each of these areas plays a crucial role in the development workflow.

The **Working Directory** is where you make changes to your project files. It represents the project's current state as it exists on your file system. When you create, modify, or delete files, these actions occur in the Working Directory. However, these changes are not immediately recorded by Git; they are considered untracked or modified files until explicitly managed.

The **Staging Area**, also known as the index, acts as an intermediary between the Working Directory and the Repository. When changes are staged, they are placed in the Staging Area. This area allows you to selectively choose which changes you want to commit, offering granular control over the development process. Staging changes does not yet make them part of the project history; it simply marks them for inclusion in the next commit.

The **Repository** is the collection of all commits and historical records. It contains the complete history of the project, including changes made, when they were made, and who made them. The Repository is stored in the .git directory, which includes compressed object files, references (such as branches and tags), and configurations.

To elucidate this process, consider the following workflow example. Suppose you are working on a project and you create a new file named newfile.txt in the Working Directory. To bring this new file under Git tracking, you would follow these steps:

- First, check the status of your Working Directory to see any untracked files.

```
$ git status
On branch main

No commits yet

Untracked files:
  (use "git add <file>..." to include in what will be committed)
        newfile.txt

nothing added to commit but untracked files present (use "git add" to track)
```

  The output indicates that newfile.txt is untracked.

- Next, add the file to the Staging Area using the git add command.

```
$ git add newfile.txt
```

  Now, check the status again to confirm that the file has been staged.

```
$ git status
On branch main

No commits yet

Changes to be committed:
  (use "git rm --cached <file>..." to unstage)
        new file: newfile.txt
```

The output now shows that newfile.txt is staged and ready to be committed.

- Finally, commit the change to the Repository:

```
$ git commit -m "Add newfile.txt"
[main (root-commit) 1d4c3b4] Add newfile.txt
 1 file changed, 0 insertions(+), 0 deletions(-)
 create mode 100644 newfile.txt
```

The output indicates that the commit is successful. The file has been added to the Repository's history.

Clarity in these areas enhances effective utilization of Git's capabilities. The Working Directory is your active workspace, the Staging Area enables controlled commit preparation, and the Repository stores your project's historical data. Understanding the interaction between these components is essential for seamless version control.

3.2 Committing Changes

The commit operation in Git represents a fundamental step in the version control workflow. It captures the state of the working directory and stages the changes, thereby creating a snapshot of the project's history. Each commit provides a reference that aids in tracking the progression of a project, enabling developers to revert to previous states, compare changes, and collaborate efficiently.

A commit can be created using the git commit command. Primarily, git commit captures the staged changes in the repository with an associated commit message. It is crucial to understand that Git commits only the changes that have been staged using the git add command.

```
git commit -m "Descriptive commit message"
```

The -m flag followed by a message in quotes specifies a commit message directly from the command line. This message should succinctly describe the changes introduced in the commit, aiding in future reference and collaboration. For longer, more detailed commit messages, you may invoke the default text editor configured in Git by simply using git commit without the -m flag.

```
git commit
```

Upon executing this command, Git launches the configured text editor, prompting the user to enter a commit message. The first line typically serves as a short summary of the changes, followed by a blank line, and then a more detailed description if necessary.

- A commit in Git is identified by a unique SHA-1 hash. This hash ensures the integrity and the immutability of the commit, enabling a secure and reliable historical record. Alongside the hash, a commit also includes metadata such as the author and committer identities (including timestamps) and the commit message.

To illustrate the commit process, consider the following example: Assume you have modified a file named example.txt and added it to the staging area:

```
git add example.txt
```

Next, commit the changes with a meaningful commit message:

```
git commit -m "Update example.txt with additional content"
```

- Effective commit messages are crucial for maintaining a comprehensible project history. It is recommended to adhere to the following best practices when composing commit messages:

- Begin with a short, imperative-style summary (up to 50 characters) of the changes introduced.

- Follow the summary with a blank line.

- Provide a detailed description of the changes, explaining the what, why, and how if necessary.

An exemplary commit message might look like:

```
Add user authentication

Implement user authentication using JWT. This includes
the creation of login and signup endpoints, and the
integration of authentication middleware to protect private routes.

Fixes issue #42
```

The message effectively communicates the scope and rationale behind the changes and references related issues or tasks.

- In certain scenarios, you might realize that the commit message does not fully capture the intended description, or there are additional modifications to include. Git allows amending the last commit using the –amend option:

```
git commit --amend
```

This command opens the text editor, allowing you to edit the existing commit message. If the working directory has further changes to be included in the commit, stage those changes before running the amend command. The amended commit replaces the previous one, retaining the same parent commit.

- For enhanced security and authenticity verification, Git supports GPG-signed commits. A signed commit ensures that the commit has not been tampered with and verifies the identity of the committer.

To create a GPG-signed commit, utilize the -S flag:

```
git commit -S -m "Significant security update"
```

Ensure that GPG keys are properly configured and available for Git to utilize. Verification of signed commits can be performed at any point to validate the authenticity.

- While the typical workflow involves adding changes to the staging area before committing, Git provides a shortcut method to bypass staging:

```
git commit -a -m "Direct commit without staging"
```

The -a flag automatically stages all tracked, modified files prior to committing. It does not include new, untracked files.

Correctly utilizing commits is vital for maintaining a coherent and traceable project history. Efficient commit practices facilitate collaboration, debugging, and project management, forming the backbone of any sophisticated version control strategy in Git.

3.3 Viewing Commit History

Examining the commit history is an essential aspect of utilizing Git effectively. It helps developers track changes, understand the evolution of the project, debug issues, and collaborate more efficiently. Git provides several commands to view the commit history, each with different options and functionalities to refine the output according to specific needs.

The primary command for viewing the commit history is git log. It displays a chronological list of commits, showing essential details such as the commit hash, author information, date, and the commit message.

```
$ git log
```

By default, git log outputs a comprehensive list of commits in reverse chronological order. The output includes:

- **Commit Hash:** A 40-character SHA-1 hash uniquely identifying the commit.
- **Author:** The name and email of the individual who created the commit.
- **Date:** The date and time when the commit was made.
- **Commit Message:** The message provided by the author to describe the changes introduced in the commit.

Here is an example output of the git log command:

```
commit df5c23e5fceb1ad6fc1d88d950c4a4b7518b2b79
Author: John Doe <john.doe@example.com>
Date:   Fri Apr 1 14:23:39 2023 -0400

    Implemented user authentication feature

commit 9b1c7d33ed93b75e8cbf930c5a1b9a335048a6f3
Author: Jane Smith <jane.smith@example.com>
Date:   Thu Mar 31 10:12:15 2023 -0400

    Fixed login bug and updated README
```

While git log provides a detailed view, it may be overwhelming for large projects with extensive histories. Git offers several options to customize the output.

Limiting the Number of Commits

To view a specific number of recent commits, the -n option can be used. For example, to display the last three commits:

```
$ git log -n 3
```

Oneline Format

For a more concise view, the –oneline option condenses each commit to a single line including the commit hash and the commit message:

```
$ git log --oneline
```

Example output:

```
df5c23e Implemented user authentication feature
9b1c7d3 Fixed login bug and updated README
```

Graphical Representation

Git also allows displaying a graphical representation of the commit history using the –graph option. This is particularly useful for visualizing branches and merges.

```
$ git log --graph
```

Combining –graph with –oneline and –all provides a compact and comprehensive view:

```
$ git log --graph --oneline --all
```

Example output:

```
* df5c23e (HEAD -> main, origin/main) Implemented user authentication feature
* 9b1c7d3 Fixed login bug and updated README
| * 4e5f6a3 (feature-branch) Added user profile page
|/
* 7a8b9c2 Initial commit
```

Custom Format

For further customization, the –pretty option allows specifying a custom format. For instance, to show only the commit hash and commit message:

```
$ git log --pretty=format:"%h - %s"
```

In this format:

- %h represents the abbreviated commit hash.
- %s represents the commit message.

Example output:

```
df5c23e - Implemented user authentication feature
9b1c7d3 - Fixed login bug and updated README
```

Filtering by Author

To filter commits made by a specific author, the –author option can be used:

```
$ git log --author="John Doe"
```

Filtering by Date

Similarly, the –since and –until options allow filtering commits within a specific date range:

```
$ git log --since="2023-03-01" --until="2023-03-31"
```

Showing Differences

To include the differences introduced by each commit in the output, the -p option can be used. This shows the diff for each commit along with the usual log information:

```
$ git log -p
```

Given the versatile range of options provided by Git for viewing commit history, users can tailor their commands to extract the most relevant and useful information for their specific needs. Understanding these options fosters better insight into project development and aids in efficient collaboration among team members.

3.4 Understanding and Creating Git Ignore Files

A crucial aspect of managing a Git repository involves deciding which files should be tracked by Git and which should be ignored. This can be effectively managed using Git ignore files. Git ignore files are special files that tell Git which files or directories to ignore in a repository. This section elaborates on the purpose, structure, and usage of .gitignore files.

The primary reason for ignoring certain files is to avoid unnecessary clutter in the repository. For instance, files generated by the operating system, compiled or binary files, and local configuration files are typically not useful for tracking changes and should not be committed to the repository. By listing these files in a .gitignore file, Git will know to skip them during the tracking process.

The .gitignore file uses a syntax that represents patterns of file names. When a file matches a pattern in the .gitignore file, Git will ignore it. To create and manage this file, it involves a few straightforward steps.

Creating a .gitignore file can be done in the root directory of your repository. The file can be named .gitignore and saved in the project root directory. Here is an example:

```
touch .gitignore
```

Once the .gitignore file is created, you can open it with a text editor and add the files and directories to be ignored. Each line in the file specifies a pattern for files or directories to be ignored. Below is an example of a .gitignore file:

```
# Ignore object files and compiled binaries
*.o
*.a
*.slo
*.lo
*.la
*.out

# Ignore build directories
/build/
/*.build/

# Ignore log files
*.log

# Ignore temporary and backup files
*~
*.bak
*.swp
```

In the example above, the .gitignore file instructs Git to ignore all object files (with extensions .o, .a), compiled binaries (with extensions .slo, .lo, .la, .out), all files within directories named "build", all files with a .log extension, and temporary or backup files whose names match the specified patterns.

The patterns used in .gitignore follow globbing rules:

- * matches any number of characters within a filename.
- ? matches a single character.
- ** matches directories recursively.
- A leading slash / matches the pattern only at the root of the project.

- A trailing slash / indicates a directory.

For example:

```
# Ignore all files ending with .log in any directory
*.log

# Ignore only the files ending with .log at the root directory
/*.log

# Ignore all .log files in the "logs" directory and its subdirectories
logs/**/*.log
```

To ensure your .gitignore patterns work as expected, you can list ignored files using the following command:

```
git ls-files --others --ignored --exclude-standard
```

This command will list all the files that are ignored by Git based on the patterns in the .gitignore file.

Remember that Git only respects the .gitignore file if the rules are added before the files are introduced into the version control. If a file has already been tracked by Git, adding it to .gitignore will not make Git stop tracking it. To stop tracking a file that is already tracked, you first need to remove it from the repository:

```
git rm --cached <filename>
```

After running the command, the file will be removed from the staging area, but it will still be present in the working directory. Then, you can add the file pattern to the .gitignore file to ensure it is ignored in future tracking.

The effectiveness of a .gitignore file can often be enhanced by leveraging templates specific to the types of projects you're working on. For instance, there are readily available .gitignore templates for different programming languages and platforms. These templates cover common files to be ignored in typical project setups. GitHub's gitignore repository, found at https://github.com/github/gitignore, provides a comprehensive collection of .gitignore templates for various languages and project types.

Understanding and creating .gitignore files is quintessential for maintaining a clean and efficient Git repository. By judiciously ignoring unnecessary files, developers can ensure that their repositories remain uncluttered and focused on essential source code and configuration files.

3.5 Staging and Unstaging Changes

The Git version control system operates through an essential flow involving three primary areas: the working directory, the staging area (also known as the index), and the repository. Understanding how changes transition between these areas is crucial to efficient Git usage. This section focuses on the processes of staging and unstaging changes, detailing the commands and their respective roles within Git.

When a file is modified in the working directory, it must be explicitly added to the staging area before it can be committed to the repository. The command used to add files to the staging area is:

```
git add <file_path>
```

For example, to stage a file named example.txt, you would use:

```
git add example.txt
```

This command updates the index with the current content found in the working directory for the specified file. To stage all modified files, the -A option can be used:

```
git add -A
```

It is worth noting that the git add command can also be used to stage files for the first time, thereby adding them to the repository in subsequent commits.

Upon staging, it becomes possible to inspect the status of the staged changes against the working directory using the git status command. The output will typically highlight which files are staged for the next commit:

```
git status
```

Inspecting the changes can be further refined by utilizing the git diff command to show differences in staged files:

```
git diff --cached
```

The –cached option allows users to see the changes that are staged and ready to be committed.

Unstaging a file removes it from the index, effectively resetting its state to that of the working directory without altering the actual file content. The command for unstaging is:

```
git reset HEAD <file_path>
```

For instance, to unstage example.txt, you would execute:

```
git reset HEAD example.txt
```

This command reverts the index to the state of the HEAD commit for the given file, diminishing its alignment with the next commit. The HEAD in this context refers to the latest commit on the current branch.

Staging and unstaging changes can also be carried out selectively on file chunks rather than entire files, using the -p flag with git add and git reset. This interactive mode allows users to stage and unstage specific parts of files independently:

```
git add -p
```

The interactive mode walks the user through each hunk of changes and prompts for action, offering commands to stage (yes), skip (no), or edit the hunk. Similarly, the command for interactive unstaging is:

```
git reset -p
```

While the git reset command is commonly used for unstaging changes, it can also alter committed history. An understanding of its broader implications concerning commit history alteration is advanced and covered in subsequent chapters.

In situations where files in the working directory do not need to be tracked or staged, the .gitignore file is employed. Direct manipulation within the staging area can be fine-tuned using the git rm –cached command to remove tracked files from the index without deleting the actual files from the working directory:

```
git rm --cached <file_path>
```

This effectively keeps files untracked in the repository despite their presence in the working directory.

The seamless transition of updates from the working directory to the staging area, and understanding the distinction of unstaging when necessary, fortifies the repository's integrity. By mastering these commands, users optimize their version control, ensuring precise commits and effective history tracking.

3.6 Inspecting Changes with Git Diff

The *git diff* command is a powerful tool in Git, utilized for investigating the differences between various states of the repository. This includes changes between the working directory and the staging area, differences between the staging area and the last commit, and comparisons between commits. Understanding how to effectively use *git diff* can significantly enhance your ability to manage and track changes within a project.

The core functionality of *git diff* allows one to see the changes that have been made but not yet staged. By executing the following command, you can observe the modifications in the working directory that are not yet part of the staging area:

```
git diff
```

The output of this command lists the differences between the working directory and the staging area. It uses the unified diff format, which shows added and removed lines. Lines that are added are prefixed with a '+', while lines that are removed are prefixed with a '-'.

If you want to see the differences between what is staged and the last commit, you can use the *–staged* or *–cached* flag:

```
git diff --staged
```

or

```
git diff --cached
```

Both commands achieve the same result: displaying the changes that have been staged but not yet committed. This is particularly useful for reviewing changes before making a commit.

Git also allows you to compare changes between two commits. This can be done by specifying the commit hashes. For instance, to compare the differences between commit *A* and commit *B*, the following command is used:

```
git diff commitA commitB
```

Here, *commitA* and *commitB* should be replaced with the actual commit hashes or references involved. Additionally, you can use branch names or tags in place of commit hashes to compare their differences.

For more granular comparisons, such as inspecting changes in a specific file or directory, Git offers the ability to focus the diff output on specific paths. For example:

```
git diff path/to/file
```

This restricts the diff output to changes made in the specified file. Moreover, you can explore the differences in a specific file between two commits using:

```
git diff commitA commitB path/to/file
```

Git also supports various diff output formats. By default, *git diff* produces a unified diff, but this can be changed with options like *format names*, which provide different views of the changes. For instance, the *–name-only* flag lists the filenames that have differences without showing the actual changes:

```
git diff --name-only
```

Similarly, the *–name-status* flag provides a brief summary of the file changes:

```
git diff --name-status
```

This displays the file's status alongside its name: added (A), modified (M), or deleted (D).

In addition to these basic diff checks, Git provides the ability to ignore white-space changes during difference inspections. This can be useful for codebases where formatting changes (like indentation) may obscure meaningful modifications. The *–ignore-space-change* and *–ignore-all-space* flags help in such cases:

```
git diff --ignore-space-change
```

```
git diff --ignore-all-space
```

These flags are instrumental in filtering out noise due to space changes, enabling a clearer view of the actual code modifications.

The *git diff* command's versatility is further illustrated by its integration with other Git tools. For instance, it can be combined with the *git log* command to inspect changes over a series of commits. Using *git log* with the *–patch* or *-p* option:

```
git log -p
```

This displays the commit history along with the diffs for each commit, providing a chronological view of the project's changes.

Finally, graphical interfaces and tools like *gitk* or *Git Extensions* often incorporate the diff capabilities of Git, allowing users to visually explore differences between commits, branches, and the working tree in a more intuitive format.

Understanding and leveraging the *git diff* command in these varied contexts is crucial for efficient version control management in Git. This foundational knowledge enables accurate tracking, clear change reviews, and enhanced collaboration within development teams.

3.7 Reverting Changes

Reverting changes is an essential aspect of version control, allowing developers to undo modifications in a codebase. In Git, several commands and approaches enable the reversal of changes depending on the context and requirement. This section examines these methods extensively, providing practical examples to solidify understanding.

Three primary scenarios typically necessitate reverting changes:

- Undoing committed changes.
- Reverting uncommitted changes in the working directory or staging area.
- Undoing changes that are both staged and committed.

Undoing Committed Changes

To revert committed changes, developers often use git revert and git reset. The choice between these commands depends on whether a new commit for the reversal is preferred (git revert) or if a clean rewrite of the history is acceptable (git reset).

Reverting a Single Commit:

The git revert command generates a new commit that undoes the changes of a specified commit.

```
git revert <commit_hash>
```

For example, to revert commit abc1234, the following command is used:

```
git revert abc1234
```

This generates a new commit with the inverse of abc1234's changes. It's useful in collaborative environments since it maintains the commit history.

Resetting to a Previous State:

The git reset command modifies the commit history; thus, it should be used cautiously, particularly in shared repositories.

```
git reset --hard <commit_hash>
```

For example, to reset the repository to the state of commit def5678, execute:

```
git reset --hard def5678
```

This command discards all subsequent changes after def5678.

Undoing Uncommitted Changes

Changes that have not yet been committed can be reverted using different commands based on whether the changes need clearing from the working directory or the staging area.

Reverting Changes in the Working Directory:

To discard modifications to tracked files in the working directory:

```
git checkout -- <file_name>
```

As an example, to revert edits to example.txt:

```
git checkout -- example.txt
```

This reverts example.txt to its last committed state, discarding uncommitted changes.

Reverting Changes in the Staging Area:

To remove files from the staging area without affecting the working directory, use:

```
git reset HEAD <file_name>
```

For example, unstage example.txt:

```
git reset HEAD example.txt
```

This command unstages example.txt but preserves the file's modifications in the working directory.

Combining Reset and Checkout:

Sometimes, combining git reset and git checkout is necessary to fully revert a file both from the staging area and the working directory:

```
git reset HEAD <file_name>
git checkout -- <file_name>
```

For instance, to completely revert example.txt:

```
git reset HEAD example.txt
git checkout -- example.txt
```

Interactive Reverting:

Git allows interactive staging and unstaging, providing precision control over what changes to revert using git add -p and git reset -p.

To revert selected changes within a file interactively:

```
git reset -p
```

This launches an interactive prompt, allowing specific modification hunks to be unstaged.

For example, running git reset -p might display:

```
diff --git a/example.txt b/example.txt
index 1234567..7654321 100644
--- a/example.txt
+++ b/example.txt
@@ -1,3 +1,3 @@
 This is a sample file.
+New line added.
 Another line.
Stage this hunk [y,n,q,a,d,/,j,J,g,e,?]?
```

Selecting n will prevent the hunk from being unstaged.

Thus, understanding and applying these approaches ensure efficient and effective version control management in Git, allowing changes to be reverted with precision, maintaining project integrity and collaboration smoothness.

3.8 Deleting Files and Directories

In Git, deleting files and directories is a straightforward task that can be managed efficiently through specific commands. It is important to ensure that deletions are tracked properly to maintain an accurate project history and facilitate effective collaboration.

To delete a file in Git, the command git rm is used. This command not only removes the file from the working directory but also stages the deletion for the next commit. The syntax is as follows:

```
git rm <filename>
```

For instance, if there is a file named example.txt that needs to be deleted, the command would be:

```
git rm example.txt
```

Executing this command will result in the file being removed from the working directory and the change being staged. This can be verified using the git status command:

```
On branch main
Changes to be committed:
  (use "git restore --staged <file>..." to unstage)
        deleted:    example.txt
```

It is important to commit the changes after staging the deletion to finalize the operation. This is achieved using:

```
git commit -m "Delete example.txt"
```

In some cases, there might be multiple files that need to be deleted. Git simplifies this process by allowing the use of wildcard characters. For example, to delete all *.log files in the current directory, the command would be:

```
git rm *.log
```

When directories need to be deleted, the process is similar but requires the inclusion of the -r (recursive) option to ensure all contents within the directory are also removed. For example, to delete a directory named old_files, the command would be:

```
git rm -r old_files
```

It is crucial to note that git rm is only necessary for files and directories that are already being tracked by Git. If a file or directory is created and then deleted before it has ever been committed, simply deleting it from the working directory and ensuring it is not staged or committed suffices.

There are scenarios where you might want to remove files from the repository without deleting them from the local working directory. This can be accomplished using the –cached option, which stages the removal from the repository but retains the files locally. This option is particularly useful for removal of files that should no longer be tracked by Git but are necessary for local development. The syntax is:

```
git rm --cached <filename>
```

For example, to remove config.json from the repository while keeping it in the local directory, the command would be:

```
git rm --cached config.json
```

To complete this task, commit the changes as usual:

```
git commit -m "Remove config.json from repository"
```

Lastly, it is important to be cautious with deletion operations, especially in collaborative environments. Deleting files or directories that other collaborators depend on can disrupt their workflow. Always communicate significant deletions and ensure they are aligned with the project's requirements.

Through effective use of Git commands for deleting files and directories, the project repository remains clean and organized, reflecting only the necessary components for the development process.

3.9 Renaming and Moving Files

Renaming and moving files within a Git repository are essential operations that help in maintaining a well-organized and understandable project structure. Git tracks these operations efficiently while preserving the file history, ensuring that no information is lost during the transition. This section elucidates the commands and processes involved in renaming and moving files using Git, focusing on practical applications and underlying mechanics.

The primary Git command used for renaming and moving files is the git mv command. This command combines the operations of renaming (or moving) the file in the working directory and staging the change in the index.

```
git mv oldfilename newfilename
```

When you execute this command, Git carries out two actions concurrently:

- The file is renamed (or moved) in the working directory.
- The change is staged in the index, ready for the next commit.

To understand this, consider a file named example.txt that you wish to rename to sample.txt. The command would be:

```
git mv example.txt sample.txt
```

This command instantly updates the working directory and the staging area. You can verify these changes using git status, which will show that example.txt has been removed and sample.txt is a new file ready to be committed. To finalize the renaming, the changes must be committed:

```
git commit -m "Renamed example.txt to sample.txt"
```

Moving files to a different directory within the repository involves similar steps. Suppose you have a file named main.c in the root directory, and you need to move it to a directory named src:

```
git mv main.c src/main.c
```

If the src directory does not exist, it will be automatically created. Again, check the status and commit the move:

```
git commit -m "Moved main.c to src/"
```

It is crucial to highlight that Git tracks renames and moves not by comparing the file names or paths but by examining the content. This content-based tracking is why Git can follow the history of files even after they have been renamed or moved. This feature becomes particularly useful when performing log inspections, as the command git log will still display the file's history, inclusive of its old and new incarnations.

In some cases, you might choose to rename or move files manually in the file system instead of using git mv. Although feasible, this approach requires additional steps to ensure that Git correctly registers the changes. First, manually rename or move the file using your operating system's file management tools. Next, follow this with the remove (rm) and add (add) commands to update the index:

```
mv oldfilename newfilename
git rm oldfilename
git add newfilename
```

Following this, commit the changes:

```
git commit -m "Manually renamed oldfilename to newfilename"
```

Although git mv is more straightforward, understanding the manual approach is beneficial, particularly when dealing with complex scenarios or when git mv encounters issues.

To summarize, renaming and moving files in Git is a streamlined process that maintains an organized repository structure and preserves file history. Properly using the git mv command simplifies these tasks, ensuring efficient file management and tracking.

3.10 Using Git Log Effectively

The git log command is a powerful tool that allows developers to explore the commit history of a Git repository. By examining the commit logs, one can discern the sequence of modifications, identify contributors, and track changes over time. Mastering the use of git log involves understanding how to employ various options and filters to sift through the commit history effectively.

A basic invocation of the git log command presents a chronological list of commits, starting from the most recent. The default format displays the commit hash, author, date, and commit message:

```
$ git log
commit 3e1b4123c2a29f1f1d123e3f8bc9e0b1b1e7c45c
Author: Jane Doe <jane.doe@example.com>
Date: Mon Jan 10 12:34:56 2023 -0500

    Fix issue with user authentication

commit 7a2b412eb8c98418e9d18b8b8b168f50f1a2c50a
Author: John Smith <john.smith@example.com>
Date: Sun Jan 9 15:22:14 2023 -0500

    Add new feature to dashboard
```

Despite its simplicity, the default output of git log may become overwhelming for large projects. Therefore, utilizing custom flags and options to filter and format the log output is crucial.

To limit the number of commits displayed, the -n option can be used, where n is any integer. For instance, to show the last five commits:

```
$ git log -5
```

To view a concise summary of each commit, the –oneline option concatenates the commit hash and the commit message into a single line per commit:

```
$ git log --oneline
3e1b412 Fix issue with user authentication
7a2b412 Add new feature to dashboard
```

For an even more filtered output, the –author flag can be employed to view commits by a specific author:

```
$ git log --author="Jane Doe"
commit 3e1b4123c2a29f1f1d123e3f8bc9e0b1b1e7c45c
Author: Jane Doe <jane.doe@example.com>
Date: Mon Jan 10 12:34:56 2023 -0500

    Fix issue with user authentication
```

Additionally, the –since and –until flags assist in narrowing the commits by a specific date range. For example, to show commits made in the past week:

```
$ git log --since="1 week ago"
```

Combining these options results in a highly customizable log output. Consider the necessity of reviewing feature updates by a particular author over a specified time frame:

```
$ git log --author="John Smith" --since="2023-01-01" --until="2023-01-07" --oneline
```

The –grep option searches commit messages for specific keywords. If the goal is to locate commits related to a specific feature, such as "dashboard":

```
$ git log --grep="dashboard"
commit 7a2b412eb8c98418e9d18b8b8b168f50f1a2c50a
Author: John Smith <john.smith@example.com>
Date: Sun Jan 9 15:22:14 2023 -0500

    Add new feature to dashboard
```

Complex queries can be achieved by combining search terms. For example, to find commits matching either "bugfix" or "issue":

```
$ git log --grep="bugfix" --grep="issue"
```

Furthermore, the association between branches and merges can be detailed with the –graph option, visually representing the branch structure and merge history:

```
$ git log --graph --oneline
* 3e1b412 Merge branch 'feature/login'
|\
| * 3c1d2b1 Add login functionality
* | 7a2b412 Add new feature to dashboard
|/
```

For a more verbose output, –stat provides a succinct summary of file changes associated with each commit:

```
$ git log --stat
commit 3e1b4123c2a29f1f1d123e3f8bc9e0b1b1e7c45c
Author: Jane Doe <jane.doe@example.com>
Date: Mon Jan 10 12:34:56 2023 -0500

    Fix issue with user authentication

 src/auth.py | 10 +++++++---
 1 file changed, 7 insertions(+), 3 deletions(-)

commit 7a2b412eb8c98418e9d18b8b8b168f50f1a2c50a
Author: John Smith <john.smith@example.com>
Date: Sun Jan 9 15:22:14 2023 -0500

    Add new feature to dashboard

 src/dashboard.py | 22 ++++++++++------------
 1 file changed, 10 insertions(+), 12 deletions(-)
```

Ultimately, a fundamental comprehension and proficient use of git log empower developers to maintain clarity and control over a repository's history. The combination of diverse options and filters tailors the command's output to the user's specific requirements, making git log an indispensable tool for effective version control management.

Chapter 4

Branching and Merging

This chapter focuses on the concepts of branching and merging in Git, detailing how to create, switch, and view branches. It explains the process of merging branches and resolving any resulting conflicts. The chapter also explores best practices for branch management and introduces advanced topics such as cherry-picking commits, stashing changes, and rebasing branches. Additionally, it covers the use of tags for marking important points in the project history.

4.1 Introduction to Branching

Branching is a fundamental concept in Git that allows for divergent development paths within a repository. A branch in Git represents an independent line of development, facilitating multiple workflows and enabling several contributors to work on different features or bug fixes simultaneously. This section aims to demystify the concept of branches and explain why they are essential in modern software development practices.

A branch in Git is essentially a lightweight movable pointer to a commit. By default, every Git repository starts with a branch named master (or main in more recent versions). Commits in Git form a directed acyclic graph (DAG), where each commit points to its parent(s). When a new commit is created, the branch pointer moves forward to reference this new commit. This is how the history of commits is tracked on a branch.

To illustrate, consider a linear sequence of commits in a repository:

```
A --- B --- C --- D
```

Here, A, B, C, and D are sequential commits in the history. Suppose our current branch, main, points to commit D. Now, if we create a new branch, say feature, it will also point to D:

```
      D (main, feature)
     /
C ---
```

At this point, both branches are identical. However, as development continues on the feature branch, new commits will only advance the feature branch pointer, leaving the main branch pointer at commit D. For example, after two new commits on the feature branch, the history would look like:

```
      D (main)
     /
C ---
     \
      E --- F (feature)
```

Branches in Git are dynamic and can be created, deleted, and merged as needed. This flexibility allows for workflows such as feature branching, where new features are developed in isolated branches and merged back into the main branch once ready.

Creating a branch in Git is a straightforward process using the git branch command:

```
git branch feature
```

This command creates a new branch named feature, which points to the current commit. To switch to the newly created branch, the git checkout command is used:

```
git checkout feature
```

Alternatively, the git switch command can also be used to switch branches:

```
git switch feature
```

Combining branch creation and switching into a single step can be achieved with the git checkout -b or git switch -c commands:

```
git checkout -b feature
```

```
git switch -c feature
```

Branching is not only useful for feature development but also for isolating bug fixes, experimenting with new ideas, or even creating hotfixes in a production environment. By working in separate branches for each task, developers can work independently without interfering with the main codebase.

To view all branches in a repository, the git branch command without any arguments lists all local branches:

```
git branch
```

The currently active branch is highlighted with an asterisk:

```
* feature
  main
```

Remote branches, which are branches in remote repositories, can be listed using:

```
git branch -r
```

Branches that are both local and remote can be displayed using:

```
git branch -a
```

Proper branch naming conventions and branch management policies are critical in larger teams and projects. Typically, branches are named based on their purpose, such as feature/feature_name, bugfix/issue_number, or hotfix/issue_number. This structured approach aids in identifying the branch purpose and improves collaboration within teams.

```
git branch feature/login
git branch bugfix/123
git branch hotfix/456
```

Each of these branches may contain different sets of changes. Once the work on a branch is completed, it can be merged back into the main branch or any other branch as required.

In summary, branches in Git serve as an essential mechanism for parallel development and effective version control. They enable isolated environments for different tasks, enhancing productivity and reducing the risk of introducing errors into the main codebase.

4.2 Creating and Switching Branches

A branch in Git represents an independent line of development. It allows you to diverge from the main codebase (usually referred to as the main or master branch) to work on features, fixes, or experiments without affecting the stable code. Creating and switching branches in Git involves several commands that facilitate parallel development and smooth integration once the changes are finalized.

To create a new branch, the git branch command is utilized. For creating a branch named feature-xyz, execute the following command:

```
git branch feature-xyz
```

This command creates a new branch called feature-xyz from the current commit but does not switch to it. To switch to the newly created branch, use the git checkout command:

```
git checkout feature-xyz
```

Starting from Git version 2.23, an easier and more intuitive command, git switch, can be used to switch branches:

```
git switch feature-xyz
```

For convenience, the branching creation and switching can be combined into a single step using the checkout command with the -b option:

```
git checkout -b feature-xyz
```

Or using the switch command with the -c option:

```
git switch -c feature-xyz
```

To verify which branch you are currently on, use:

```
git branch
```

The output indicates the current branch with an asterisk:

```
* feature-xyz
  main
```

This indicates that feature-xyz is the active branch, and any commits made will be associated with it.

To switch back to the main branch, use:

```
git switch main
```

Or the older form:

```
git checkout main
```

When working on multiple branches, it is essential to commit your changes before switching branches to avoid losing work. If there are uncommitted changes, Git will either preserve them (in the working directory) or refuse to switch if the changes would conflict. Thus, it is good practice to regularly commit changes and use the git stash mechanism when you must switch branches with ongoing work.

Creating and switching branches are fundamental operations in collaborative and solo development workflows. It allows developers to segregate work on specific features or issues while maintaining a clean main branch for production or release purposes. These practices are paramount for maintaining a stable and manageable codebase.

4.3 Viewing Branch History

Understanding the history of changes within a branch is crucial for effective version control and collaboration. Git provides a variety of tools and commands to help inspect your branch's history. In this section, we will explore these tools and demonstrate how to use them to gain insights into the changes made over time.

To begin, the primary command for viewing the commit history in Git is git log. This command displays a list of commits on your current branch or any other specified branch.

```
git log
```

Executing git log presents a sequential list of commits starting from the most recent commit. Each entry includes the commit hash, author information, date, and commit message:

```
commit e30c4f74a8f4d131bf15b6ffee9f8c9eca713d0a
Author: John Doe <john.doe@example.com>
Date:   Tue Oct 1 12:34:56 2023 -0700

    Updated README with installation instructions
```

The git log command supports multiple options to filter and format the displayed information. For example, to view commits by a specific author, the –author flag can be employed.

```
git log --author="John Doe"
```

Sometimes, the output of git log can be too verbose for practical usage. To simplify the visualization of branch history, Git provides several options to format the log output. The –oneline option condenses each commit to a single line, showcasing only the commit hash and the commit message.

```
git log --oneline
```

```
e30c4f7 Updated README with installation instructions
d1a2b3c Fixed bug in user authentication module
c4d5e6f Initial commit
```

For a more graphical representation, the –graph option displays the branch structure and merges visually:

```
git log --graph --oneline
```

```
* e30c4f7 Updated README with installation instructions
* d1a2b3c Fixed bug in user authentication module
| * abcdef0 Merged feature branch 'new-feature'
|/
* c4d5e6f Initial commit
```

Combining useful options can yield even more information-rich logs. Using –graph, –decorate, and –all options together, one can visualize commit history with references and branches:

```
git log --graph --decorate --all
```

```
* e30c4f7 (HEAD -> master, origin/master) Updated README with installation instructions
| * abcdef0 (origin/new-feature) Merged feature branch 'new-feature'
|/
* c4d5e6f Initial commit
```

For specific file history, the git log command accepts a file path:

```
git log -- <file_path>
```

This command filters the commits affecting the specified file, which is useful for tracking changes to particular files over time.

Another powerful tool is gitk, a graphical repository browser that provides an intuitive interface to examine the commit history. To open gitk, simply type:

```
gitk
```

Additionally, gitk supports command-line options to filter and display specific branches or commits.

The git reflog command is useful for viewing the history of HEAD references, including those not listed as part of the standard commit history.

This tool allows you to recover lost commits or branches if needed.

```
git reflog
```

```
e30c4f7 HEAD@{0}: commit: Updated README with installation instructions
d1a2b3c HEAD@{1}: commit: Fixed bug in user authentication module
c4d5e6f HEAD@{2}: commit (initial): Initial commit
```

Understanding these commands and options allows for efficient navigation and inspection of branch history, enabling informed decision-making and effective collaboration. These tools provide comprehensive insights into your project's evolution, facilitating better version control practices.

4.4 Merging Branches

In Git, merging is a fundamental operation that combines changes from different branches into a single branch. When working in a collaborative environment or even on different features independently, merging helps integrate your work into the mainline branch. Merging ensures that all contributors' changes are aggregated and is crucial for maintaining a coherent project history.

To perform a merge in Git, one must first have two branches: the branch into which the changes are to be merged (the current branch) and the branch that contains the changes intended for merging. Git uses the git merge command to accomplish this task. The general syntax for the merge command is as follows:

```
git merge <branch-name>
```

Executing the above command merges the specified branch (<branch-name>) into the current branch. It is essential to understand that the order of merging operations can have a significant impact on the project history and resulting merge conflicts. Therefore, it's imperative to follow best practices for branching and merging discussed later in this chapter.

Fast-Forward Merges

When the branch to be merged is ahead of the current branch (i.e., the current branch has no new commits since the diverged point), Git performs a fast-forward merge by default. In such a scenario, the current branch pointer is simply moved forward along the commit history, as illustrated in the example below:

```
# Assume you are on the 'main' branch and want to merge the 'feature' branch
git checkout main
git merge feature
```

If the commit history of feature is linear and can be appended to the main branch without conflicts, Git moves the main branch pointer forward, incorporating the new commits.

Three-Way Merge

A three-way merge occurs when the current branch and the branch to be merged have diverged, each containing unique commits. Git uses a common ancestor, the latest commit shared by both branches, to perform the merge. During this type of merge, Git combines changes from both branches, creating a new commit that reflects the integrated history. The process of a three-way merge is depicted in the following sequence:

```
# Make sure you are on the current branch
git checkout main
# Merge the specified branch
git merge feature
```

In this example, if the feature branch contains unique commits that do not exist in the main branch and vice versa, Git creates a new commit in the main branch that includes changes from both branches.

Merge Conflicts

Merge conflicts arise when changes made in different branches affect the same lines of a file or the same section of the project in incompatible ways. Git tries to automatically merge changes; however, when it encounters conflicts, it pauses for user intervention. To resolve merge conflicts:

- Open the conflicted files in a text editor.
- Look for conflict markers that Git inserts into the files:

```
<<<<<<< HEAD
// changes from the current branch
=======
# changes from the branch being merged
>>>>>>> feature
```

- Manually edit the file to resolve the conflicting changes.
- After resolving conflicts, mark the files as resolved with:

```
git add <resolved-file>
```

- Complete the merge process by committing the changes, if required:

```
git commit
```

Merge Strategies

Depending on the project requirements, Git offers different merge strategies. The most common are recursive (default), octopus, and ours. Understanding these strategies helps in managing complex merges:

- recursive: Suitable for two branches, it performs a three-way merge.
- octopus: Used for merging more than two branches at once.
- ours: Ignores changes from other branches and effectively keeps the current branch's content.

You can specify a merge strategy using the -s option:

```
git merge -s recursive <branch-name>
```

Proper merging helps maintain a clean and consistent project history, reducing complications in collaborative development.

4.5 Handling Merge Conflicts

When merging branches in Git, conflicts can occur if changes in one branch are incompatible with changes in another. This section provides an in-depth exploration of how to handle these conflicts efficiently and effectively.

A merge conflict typically arises during the execution of the git merge command. When Git identifies conflicting changes in the content of files from the merging branches, it suspends the merge process, allowing the developer to manually resolve the discrepancy. Familiarizing oneself with the conflict identification and resolution process is crucial for maintaining code integrity and project progress.

Suppose we have two branches, feature-1 and main, both with changes to a common file, example.txt. Here is a step-by-step process to manage and resolve a conflict generated by merging feature-1 into main.

- **Initiate the Merge:** Begin by merging feature-1 into main.

```
git checkout main
git merge feature-1
```

  If a conflict exists, Git will provide output indicating the problematic files:

```
CONFLICT (content): Merge conflict in example.txt
Automatic merge failed; fix conflicts and then commit the result.
```

- **Identify the Conflict:** Open the conflicted file example.txt in a text editor. Git will annotate the file with conflict markers:

```
<<<<<<< HEAD
This is the content from the main branch.
=======
This is the content from the feature-1 branch.
>>>>>>> feature-1
```

  The text between «««< HEAD and ======= is from the current branch (main), while the text between ======= and »»»> feature-1 is from the branch being merged (feature-1).

- **Resolve the Conflict:** Manually edit the file to reflect the desired content. Here is an example of a conflict resolution:

```
git checkout main
git merge feature-1
```

  After resolving the conflict, the edited example.txt might look like:

```
This is the combined content from both main and feature-1 branches.
```

- **Mark the Conflict as Resolved:** Once the conflicts are resolved, the next step is to mark the file as resolved and complete the merge process. This is done using the following commands:

```
git add example.txt
git commit -m "Resolved merge conflict between main and feature-1"
```

- **Test the Resolution:** It is prudent to thoroughly test the project to ensure that the resolution has not inadvertently introduced bugs or inconsistencies. Comprehensive testing helps verify the correctness and stability of the integrated changes.

In addition to the manual resolution process outlined above, Git offers various tools to assist in conflict resolution. These include built-in merge tools and external tools integrated with Git. To set a default merge tool, configure Git with the following command:

```
git config --global merge.tool <toolname>
```

Replace <toolname> with the name of the merge tool you intend to use, such as kdiff3, meld, or vimdiff. Use the configured merge tool by invoking:

```
git mergetool
```

The selected merge tool will present a visual interface for resolving conflicts, facilitating a more streamlined and intuitive process.

Handling conflicts is not solely a technical task but also involves effective communication within the development team. Conflicts often arise due to concurrent changes that lack awareness of each other's context. Collaboration and informed synchronization can mitigate extensive conflicts.

Embracing best practices in branch management, such as regular merges, keeping branches short-lived, and frequently communicating changes within the team, can reduce the frequency and complexity of conflicts. Additionally, establishing and adhering to a consistent coding standard helps maintain uniformity in code changes, further minimizing merge conflicts.

Understanding and mastering conflict resolution is pivotal for proficient use of Git in collaborative environments, ensuring continuity and consistency in project development.

4.6 Branch Management Best Practices

Effective branch management is a critical aspect of maintaining a clean, organized, and functional Git repository. The practices outlined in this section are designed to help teams and individual developers manage their workflow efficiently, minimize conflicts, and ensure a smooth integration process.

Firstly, it is essential to understand the importance of a clear branching strategy. A common practice is to follow a model such as Gitflow, which organizes branches into well-defined categories like feature branches, develop branches, and release branches. The primary branches typically include:

- main or master: This branch contains production-ready code. It should always be stable and deployable.
- develop: This branch serves as an integration branch for features. It is where completed features are merged and tested before being included in the main branch.
- feature/*: These branches are used for developing new features. Each feature branch is derived from the develop branch and is merged back into develop when the feature is complete.
- release/*: These branches support preparation of a new production release. They allow for final bug fixing and adjustments. Once ready, these are merged into both main and develop.
- hotfix/*: These branches are for quick fixes to the production code. After the fix is ready, it is merged into both main and develop.

Branch naming conventions are vital. Consistent and descriptive names ensure that everyone can easily understand the purpose of each branch without ambiguity. For instance, a feature branch might be named feature/user-authentication, indicating it deals with a user authentication feature.

Regular branch synchronization is necessary to avoid divergence and hard-to-resolve conflicts. Developers should frequently rebase their feature branches onto the latest develop branch:

```
git checkout feature/user-authentication
git fetch origin
git rebase origin/develop
```

By rebasing often, the feature branch is kept up-to-date with the mainline development, making the final merge smoother and less prone to conflicts.

Branches should have a clearly defined scope and timeline. Features should be small and incremental, with individual branches not existing for prolonged periods. This practice lessens the likelihood of complex conflicts and simplifies code reviews. Long-lived branches often become stale and diverge significantly from the main codebase, complicating integration.

Maintaining a linear commit history is beneficial for understanding the progression of changes. The git rebase command can be used to rewrite commit history to make it linear, but it must be used carefully, especially with shared branches:

```
git checkout feature/user-authentication
git rebase -i HEAD~3
```

This command opens an interactive rebase session, allowing to squish or reorder commits. Avoid using rebase on public branches as it can rewrite shared commit history, leading to potential disruptions for other collaborators.

Periodic branch pruning is another best practice. Once branches are merged and their changes are confirmed working in the main or develop branches, they should be deleted to keep the repository tidy:

```
git branch -d feature/user-authentication
git push origin --delete feature/user-authentication
```

This deletion removes the branch both locally and remotely. An organized branch structure lowers the cognitive load on developers, who can focus on relevant branches without wading through obsolete ones.

Ensuring tests and continuous integration (CI) are in place before merging changes is crucial. CI tools can run automated tests and checks, guaranteeing the integrity of the code before it is integrated into critical branches. Use tools like Jenkins, Travis CI, or GitHub Actions in your development workflow to automate these processes.

Using pull requests (PRs) for merges promotes code review and collaborative assessment. PRs facilitate discussion, highlight potential issues, and foster code quality. A typical PR process involves:

- Creating a PR from a feature branch to the develop branch.
- Requesting reviews from team members.
- Conducting necessary corrections based on feedback.
- Automatic and manual testing of the code changes.
- Once approved, merging the PR into the develop branch.

Finally, it is imperative to document branch policies clearly in a contributing guide or repository policy document. This documentation informs all contributors about the agreed-upon workflow, ensuring consistency and reducing onboarding time for new developers.

A coherent branch management strategy streamlines development processes, maintains code quality, and facilitates collaborative work, setting a foundation for the successful operation of software projects.

4.7 Cherry-Picking Commits

Cherry-picking in Git allows you to select specific commits from one branch and apply them onto another branch. This operation is particularly useful when you need to port bug fixes or features to different branches without merging entire branches.

To cherry-pick a commit, you will use the git cherry-pick command followed by the commit hash. Consider the following scenario where the commit needs to be transferred from feature-branch to main. First, ensure that you are on the branch where you want to apply the commit:

```
git checkout main
```

Once on the main branch, execute the cherry-pick command with the specific commit's hash:

```
git cherry-pick <commit-hash>
```

Replace <commit-hash> with the actual hash value of the commit. Upon successful execution, the changes introduced by <commit-hash> will be applied to the main branch.

- **Cherry-Picking Multiple Commits**

  Cherry-picking can also be performed on multiple commits. If you have several non-contiguous commits that you need to apply, list their hashes sequentially:

  ```
  git cherry-pick <commit-hash1> <commit-hash2> <commit-hash3>
  ```

  For a range of contiguous commits, use:

  ```
  git cherry-pick <start-commit-hash>\textasciicircum..<end-commit-hash>
  ```

  The ^ character before the start hash ensures the range is inclusive of the start-commit-hash.

- **Handling Errors during Cherry-Picking**

Errors during cherry-picking can occur due to conflicts. Git will pause at the conflicting commit and require you to resolve conflicts similarly to how they are resolved during a merge. After fixing conflicts in the affected files, mark them as resolved:

```
git add <resolved-file>
```

Continue the process with:

```
git cherry-pick --continue
```

If the cherry-pick operation needs to be aborted, for instance, due to irreconcilable conflicts, it can be done using:

```
git cherry-pick --abort
```

- **Cherry-Picking with a Strategy**

  There may be situations where specifying a merge strategy is essential, particularly if the default strategy does not yield the desired outcome. The git cherry-pick command supports the -X flag to define specific strategies. For instance, to resolve merges automatically favoring the current branch when conflicts occur, use the ours strategy:

```
git cherry-pick -X ours <commit-hash>
```

  Alternatively, to favor the incoming changes:

```
git cherry-pick -X theirs <commit-hash>
```

- **Cherry-Picking in a Script**

  In more extensive workflows, cherry-picking might be automated within scripts. Careful scripting ensures commits are consistently applied, and appropriate error handling mechanisms enable a robust process. Below is a basic script to cherry-pick a commit onto the current branch:

```
#!/bin/bash

# Define commit hash
COMMIT_HASH=$1

# Cherry-pick the commit
if git cherry-pick $COMMIT_HASH; then
```

```
    echo "Cherry-pick of $COMMIT_HASH successful"
else
    echo "Cherry-pick failed, resolving conflicts if any"
    git status
    # You can handle other resolutions here
fi
```

This script takes the commit hash as an argument and attempts to cherry-pick it. If conflicts occur, it prints the current status, allowing further conflict resolution steps to be integrated.

Careful implementation of cherry-picking ensures its effectiveness in transferring selective changes across branches, maintaining the integrity and organization of the project history.

4.8 Stashing Changes

Stashing in Git is a powerful feature that allows developers to temporarily set aside their modifications without committing them. This is particularly useful when switching contexts or branches without cluttering the commit history.

The fundamental command for stashing changes is:

```
git stash
```

When this command is executed, Git saves the changes to tracked files in a stash entry and reverts the working directory to match the HEAD commit. This includes modifications in both the working directory and the index. Only tracked files are stashed. Untracked files are left unchanged by default but can be included using additional options.

To include untracked files, use the -u or –include-untracked flag:

```
git stash -u
```

For including both untracked and ignored files, use the –all flag:

```
git stash --all
```

To view the list of all stashed changes, the following command is used:

```
git stash list
```

This returns an output similar to:

```
stash@{0}: WIP on main: abc1234 Commit message
stash@{1}: WIP on feature-branch: def5678 Another commit message
```

Each stash entry is identified using stash@{index} notation where the index represents the stash's position in the list.

Applying stashed changes can be done in several ways, one of which is the git stash apply command. This applies the changes from the latest stash entry but does not remove it from the stash list:

```
git stash apply
```

To apply a specific stash entry by its index:

```
git stash apply stash@{1}
```

If the applied stash conflicts with the current state of the working directory, Git will notify about the conflicts, which need to be resolved manually.

To both apply a stash entry and remove it from the stash list, use the git stash pop command:

```
git stash pop
```

Similar to git stash apply, a specific stash entry can also be popped:

```
git stash pop stash@{1}
```

If the stashed changes are no longer needed, they can be removed from the stash list without applying. This is done using:

```
git stash drop stash@{1}
```

Or to clear all stashes at once:

```
git stash clear
```

It is essential to understand that applying or popping stashed changes might lead to potential conflicts if the working directory has diverging changes. These conflicts are to be resolved similarly to other merge conflicts.

Another useful command is git stash branch. This command creates a new branch from the state recorded in the stash and applies the latest stash entry to it:

```
git stash branch <new-branch-name>
```

The stash entry is dropped if the command completes without errors.

To stash with a message, providing context for the stash, use:

```
git stash push -m "message"
```

This message helps in identifying the stash entries, especially when working with multiple stashes.

It is important to note that files in the .gitignore list are not stashed unless explicitly included using –all. This ensures that the configurations and settings specific to the development environment are not unnecessarily stored in the stash entries.

Incorporating stashing into your workflow can significantly enhance productivity, enabling smooth transitions between tasks without losing progress. Proper understanding and management of stashed changes optimize the development cycle and maintain organized commit histories.

4.9 Rebasing Branches

Rebasing in Git is a powerful feature that allows users to streamline a series of commits, reapply commits on top of another base tip, thus maintaining a linear project history. Unlike merging, which incorporates all changes from one branch into another while preserving the history of commits, rebasing transfers the completed work from one branch and reapplies it onto another.

The primary advantage of rebasing is maintaining a cleaner, linear history, which can be particularly useful for projects where a clear progression of changes is crucial. However, rebasing should be used with caution, especially when working with shared branches, as it rewrites commit history.

Performing a Basic Rebase

To rebase a branch on top of another, use the git rebase command. For example, given branches feature and main, to rebase feature onto main, follow these steps:

```
git checkout feature
git rebase main
```

The command sequence checks out the feature branch and then rebases it onto main. This operation replays the commits from feature onto main, effectively moving the base of feature to the head of main.

Interactive Rebase

Interactive rebasing adds an additional layer of control, allowing users to edit, reorder, or squash commits. This is invoked using the -i flag:

```
git rebase -i main
```

Upon execution, an editor opens, presenting a list of commits in the form:

```
pick e4a1d12 Commit message 1
pick d1f4516 Commit message 2
pick acb4d72 Commit message 3
```

The user can replace pick with commands like edit, reword, squash, etc., to modify the commits as needed. For instance, to squash the second and third commits into the first:

```
pick e4a1d12 Commit message 1
squash d1f4516 Commit message 2
squash acb4d72 Commit message 3
```

During the rebase, Git will pause and allow the user to edit commit messages and resolve conflicts if they arise.

Handling Conflicts During Rebase

Conflicts during a rebase are resolved similarly to merge conflicts. If a conflict occurs, Git pauses the rebase process, allowing the user to fix the conflicts manually. After resolving conflicts, the following commands are necessary:

```
git add <resolved_files>
git rebase --continue
```

If the situation becomes complex or if the rebase needs to be aborted, the command is:

```
git rebase --abort
```

This command will return the branch to its original state before the rebase began.

Rebasing vs. Merging

While both rebasing and merging allow integration of changes from one branch to another, their philosophies differ:

- **Merging**: preserves the complete history, including the points of divergence and integration.
- **Rebasing**: creates a linear history by reapplying commits from one branch to another.

Rebasing is preferred for maintaining a tidy project history but should be used with caution on shared branches as it rewrites commit history and can lead to issues if others have based their work on the original branch structure.

Best Practices for Rebasing

1. **Private Branches**: Rebase only branches that are not shared with others to avoid rewriting shared commit history.
2. **Frequent Commits**: Rebase frequently to minimize conflicts and keep changes synchronized with the base branch.
3. **Review and Test**: After rebasing, review and test the code thoroughly to ensure that changes have been accurately integrated.

Force-Pushing After Rebase

Since rebasing changes commit history, pushing a rebased branch will typically require a force push:

```
git push --force
```

Force pushing should be performed cautiously, especially with branches others might be using, to avoid inadvertently overwriting other developers' work.

In projects with collaborative efforts, it is crucial to communicate and coordinate with your team when performing a rebase, ensuring everyone understands the implications and follows the necessary steps to synchronize their forks or clones.

4.10 Working with Tags

In Git, tags are a way to mark specific points in the project's history as being important. Typically, these are used to mark release points (e.g., v1.0, v2.0), but they're also useful for marking any other significant checkpoints. Tags provide a handy mechanism to remember important events in the repository's history. This section will cover the creation, listing, fetching, and deletion of tags, as well as the differences between lightweight and annotated tags.

Tags in Git come in two varieties: lightweight and annotated.

A lightweight tag is very much like a branch that doesn't change—it's just a pointer to a specific commit. To create a new lightweight tag named v1.0, you can execute the following command:

```
$ git tag v1.0
```

Annotated tags, on the other hand, are stored as full objects in the Git database. They're checksummed; contain the tagger name, email, and date; have a tagging message; and can be signed and verified via GNU Privacy Guard (GPG). In creating an annotated tag also named v1.0, you would use the -a flag and provide a message:

```
$ git tag -a v1.0 -m "Release version 1.0"
```

It is generally advisable to create annotated tags so that you can store additional metadata about the tag.

You can list tags in your repository with the following command:

```
$ git tag
```

If you want to see the tags that match a particular pattern, you can execute:

```
$ git tag -l "v1.*"
```

Retrieving specific tag information, especially for annotated tags, can be accomplished by passing the tag name to git show:

```
$ git show v1.0
```

This command will display the tag metadata and the associated commit. For example:

```
tag v1.0
Tagger: John Doe <john.doe@example.com>
Date:   Tue Apr 20 12:34:56 2021 -0700

Release version 1.0

commit abcdef1234567890abcdef1234567890abcdef12
Author: John Doe <john.doe@example.com>
Date:   Mon Apr 19 11:33:22 2021 -0700

    Initial project version
```

Sharing tags among collaborators requires pushing them to a remote repository. By default, the git push command does not transfer tags to your remote servers. You have to explicitly push tags via:

```
$ git push origin v1.0
```

Alternatively, if you want to push all tags, use:

```
$ git push origin --tags
```

Fetching tags from a remote repository can be done using:

```
$ git fetch <remote> --tags
```

Organizing and maintaining tags might also necessitate their deletion. To delete a tag locally, you can use:

```
$ git tag -d v1.0
```

If you need to remove a tag from a remote repository, ensure it is deleted locally, then push the deletion:

```
$ git push origin :refs/tags/v1.0
```

When working with tags, it is critical to consider their immutability in a collaborative environment. Tags once published should not be changed since they are meant to represent stable points in the history of the repository.

The signing of tags introduces a layer of security by proving the tag was created by a specific individual, useful in environments where the provenance of release points must be authenticated. The following command signs the tag upon creation:

```
$ git tag -s v1.0 -m "Signed release version 1.0"
```

Verification of a signed tag can be done using:

```
$ git tag -v v1.0
```

Properly utilizing tags in Git thus streamlines the management of important project milestones, ensuring a clear and efficient version history.

Chapter 5

Remote Repositories

This chapter covers the use of remote repositories in Git, starting with an explanation of their purpose and setup. It details how to configure remote URLs, fetch changes, and push updates to remote repositories. Key operations such as pulling changes and cloning remote repositories are explained. The chapter also explores concepts like forking and upstream repositories, managing multiple remotes, and understanding remote branches, providing a comprehensive guide to effectively collaborating on distributed projects.

5.1 Understanding Remote Repositories

A remote repository in Git acts as a version-controlled repository that exists on a remote server. This repository is integral to collaboration, allowing multiple users to share changes to a project without necessarily being in the same physical location. Unlike local repositories, which reside on an individual's machine, remote repositories are usually hosted on a service like GitHub, GitLab, or Bitbucket, though they can also be hosted on a private server.

Remote repositories enable several key functionalities in a distributed version control environment:

- Centralized Collaboration: Allow teams to work together on a project by providing a central repository from which every participant can push their changes or pull updates. This avoids the complexities of peer-to-peer updates and ensures that there is a single source of truth for the project's history.

- Backup and Redundancy: Serve as an off-site backup, protecting against data loss due to local machine failures. By having the project stored remotely, you mitigate risk and ensure that the development history is preserved.
- Workflow Optimization: Support advanced workflows such as continuous integration/continuous deployment (CI/CD). Automated processes can be triggered on the remote repository, such as running tests or deploying an application whenever changes are pushed.

Interaction with a remote repository typically involves several key operations, each discussed in depth within this chapter. These operations include configuring remote URLs, fetching from and pushing to a remote repository, and pulling updates. The underlying principle revolves around ensuring consistency between the local and remote states of the repository.

To understand the usage of remote repositories, it's vital to get familiar with certain fundamental commands. For instance, the git remote command is used to manage a set of tracked repositories. Here's an example to list remote repositories associated with a local repository:

```
git remote -v
```

When executed, this command might provide an output similar to:

```
origin  https://github.com/username/repo.git (fetch)
origin  https://github.com/username/repo.git (push)
```

This example output indicates that the remote repository named origin is linked via the URL https://github.com/username/repo.git for both fetching and pushing operations.

To add a new remote repository, you use the git remote add command followed by an identifier for the remote and its URL. For instance, adding a remote repository:

```
git remote add upstream https://github.com/original/repo.git
```

Here, upstream is the name given to the remote URL https://github.com/original/repo.git. Choosing descriptive names for remote repositories helps mitigate confusion, especially when dealing with multiple remotes.

Fetching updates from a remote repository is an essential part of incorporating changes made by others. The git fetch command downloads objects and refs from another repository:

```
git fetch origin
```

This command will retrieve the branches and updates from the remote named origin but does not integrate these changes with your local branches, allowing you to review before merging.

Pushing changes involves sending your committed changes to a remote repository, typically using the git push command:

```
git push origin main
```

This command sends the local branch named main to the remote repository named origin, updating it with your recent changes.

Pulling is a combination of fetching changes and merging them. The git pull command automates this process:

```
git pull origin main
```

This command fetches the latest changes from the main branch of the remote repository origin and directly integrates them into your current branch.

The underlying concept of remote repositories in Git revolves around distributed collaboration. Each user maintains their own repository, making changes and periodically synchronizing with shared remotes to integrate their contributions. This model provides robust capabilities for concurrent development, extensive branching, and a detailed history that can be accessed and manipulated locally and remotely.

5.2 Setting Up a Remote Repository

Setting up a remote repository is a fundamental task in collaborating with other developers using Git. A remote repository serves as a centralized location where team members can share code changes. This section explores the step-by-step process of setting up such a repository, assuming that you have already covered the basic Git installation and configuration.

To begin setting up a remote repository, you need access to a remote hosting service such as GitHub, GitLab, or Bitbucket. These platforms provide graphical user interfaces and additional features for managing Git repositories. For illustrative purposes, this section will guide you through setting up a remote repository on GitHub.

Step 1: Create a GitHub Account
If you do not already have a GitHub account, navigate to https://github.com and sign up. You will need to provide your email address, create a username, and set a password. Verification via email or other means might be required.

Step 2: Create a New Repository
Once you have an account and are logged in, click on the "+" icon at the top-right corner of the GitHub interface and select "New repository." You will be presented with an interface to create your new repository.

Fill in the repository details:

- **Repository Name**: A unique name for your repository.
- **Description**: (Optional) A brief description of your project.
- **Public/Private**: Choose whether the repository is public (visible to everyone) or private (visible only to you and collaborators).
- **Initialize this repository with a README**: Optionally select this to automatically include a README file.

After filling in the necessary information, click the "Create repository" button.

Step 3: Configuring the Local Repository
Assume you have a local repository on your machine. You need to link this local repository to the newly created remote repository. Open your terminal or Git Bash, and navigate to the directory containing your local repository.

Use the following Git command to add a remote repository:

```
git remote add origin https://github.com/your-username/your-repo-name.git
```

Replace your-username with your GitHub username and your-repo-name with the name of your GitHub repository.

You can verify that the remote repository has been added by executing:

```
git remote -v
```

The output should display something similar to the following:

```
origin https://github.com/your-username/your-repo-name.git (fetch)
origin https://github.com/your-username/your-repo-name.git (push)
```

This indicates that the remote named "origin" is correctly set up for both fetching and pushing.

Step 4: Push Local Changes to Remote Repository
If your local repository contains existing commits that you want to push to the newly created remote repository, you can use the following command to push the changes:

```
git push -u origin master
```

This command pushes your current branch to the remote repository and sets the upstream tracking reference. Substitute master with the name of your branch if it differs.

If you initialized the remote repository with a README file, you may encounter a "non-fast-forward" error. In that case, fetch the changes from the remote repository first:

```
git pull origin master --allow-unrelated-histories
```

Then, proceed to push your changes again.

Step 5: Collaborator Access
For collaborative projects, you may want to allow other users to contribute to your repository. Navigate to the repository page on GitHub, click "Settings," and find the "Collaborators" section. Here, you can add GitHub usernames or email addresses of your collaborators and set their access permissions (Write, Read, Admin, etc.).

By following these steps, you have successfully set up a remote repository on GitHub and linked it to your local repository. This setup allows you to push and pull changes between your local and remote repositories, facilitating collaborative development.

5.3 Configuring Remote URLs

In order to harness the full capability of Git's distributed version control system, connecting your local repository with remote repositories is paramount. Configuring remote URLs ensures communication between your local environment and remote servers, facilitating the pulling and pushing of changes essential for collaborative development.

A remote URL typically follows the syntax:

protocol://[user@]hostname/path/to/repository.git

The protocol can be one of several supported by Git, namely https, ssh, git, or ftp, among others. The hostname specifies the server where the repository resides, and the path denotes the location of the repository on that server.

To set a remote URL, the git remote add command is employed. Suppose you're working on a repository hosted on GitHub, and you wish to add a remote named origin, you would execute:

```
git remote add origin https://github.com/username/repo.git
```

Here, origin is a convenient shortcut name for the URL, making references in future commands easier.

To verify the current configuration of remote URLs, use the git remote -v command. This lists all remotes along with their respective fetch and push URLs:

```
$ git remote -v
origin https://github.com/username/repo.git (fetch)
origin https://github.com/username/repo.git (push)
```

Often, after creating a repository on a service like GitHub, you need to set the upstream remote to link the local and remote repositories. This can be done when cloning a repository or by using the git remote add command after initializing a local repository.

To update an existing remote URL, perhaps after migrating to a different hosting service or changing the repository's location, the git remote set-url command is utilized:

```
git remote set-url origin git@github.com:username/newrepo.git
```

This command is useful for modifying the remote URL without adding a new remote or re-cloning the repository. It ensures the mapping between the local repository and the remote is seamlessly updated.

Multiple remotes can be managed within a single repository. Let's consider an example where you have an upstream repository and a fork. You might want to keep track of the original repository (upstream) and the fork (origin). This can be achieved by identifying and adding remotes with descriptive names:

```
git remote add origin https://github.com/myusername/myfork.git
git remote add upstream https://github.com/originaluser/originalrepo.git
```

Here, origin points to your fork and upstream points to the repository from which the fork was created. This setup allows you to pull updates from the upstream repository and integrate them into your fork.

To rename a remote, for example, changing upstream to original, the following command is used:

```
git remote rename upstream original
```

This renaming is merely a local operation for easier reference and does not affect the remote repository.

After configuring, validating the remote setup periodically helps ensure there are no linkage issues. You can use various Git commands, such as git fetch and git pull, along with the remote name to verify operational stability.

In scenarios where the remote URL is secure and credentials are handled via the .git-credentials or via SSH keys, it's advantageous to utilize the appropriate protocol for efficiency and security. For example, switching from HTTPS to SSH configurations involves altering the URL:

```
git remote set-url origin git@github.com:username/repo.git
```

This command sets the remote origin to use SSH, assuming SSH keys are already configured on your system.

Understanding the practical intricacies of remote URL configurations plays a critical role in streamlining collaboration and ensuring smooth repository interactions within Git's distributed framework.

5.4 Fetching from a Remote Repository

Fetching is a fundamental operation in Git that allows you to update your local copy of a repository with the latest changes from a remote repository. Unlike pulling, fetching only updates the remote-tracking branches in your local repository without merging these changes into your working directory. This provides greater control and ensures that you can review changes before integrating them into your codebase.

Fetch Command and Syntax: The basic command to fetch changes from a remote repository is:

```
git fetch <remote-name>
```

The <remote-name> is typically origin, but it can be any name assigned to the remote repository during its configuration.

Example: To fetch updates from a remote repository named origin, the command would be:

```
git fetch origin
```

Upon execution, Git contacts the remote repository identified by origin and fetches data, updating your local repository's remote-tracking branches.

Verbose Option: To get more detailed information on what exactly is fetched, you can use the –verbose (or -v) option:

```
git fetch --verbose origin
```

This command provides additional details about the new commits and branches that were fetched.

Dry Run: If you want to preview the changes without actually fetching them, the –dry-run option is useful:

```
git fetch --dry-run origin
```

This will show what would be fetched without making any changes to your local repository.

Fetching All Remotes: To fetch changes from all configured remote repositories, you can use:

```
git fetch --all
```

This command will iterate over all remotes and fetch the latest changes for each one.

Common Use Cases: Fetching is often part of a workflow that involves inspecting the fetched changes before integration. Here are some typical scenarios where fetching is beneficial:

- *Inspecting Commit History*: After fetching, you might want to examine the remote branches and the new commits:

  ```
  git fetch origin
  git log origin/main
  ```

  The above commands fetch changes from the remote named origin and then display the commit history of the main branch on the remote repository.

- *Viewing Differences*: To understand how fetched changes differ from your current branch, you can use the git diff command:

```
git fetch origin
git diff origin/main
```

  This shows the differences between your current working branch and the main branch on the origin remote.

- *Updating Local Branches*: After fetching, you may want to update local branches to integrate fetched changes. This can be done using git merge or git rebase based on your preferred workflow:

```
git fetch origin
git checkout main
git merge origin/main
```

  Here, after fetching, you switch to the main branch and merge the fetched changes from origin/main.

Fetch Prune Option: Over time, remote branches may be deleted. To clean up such stale references in your local repository, use the –prune option:

```
git fetch --prune origin
```

This ensures that any branches deleted from the remote are also removed from your local repository's reference.

Advanced Fetching: For more specific fetching needs, you can specify a particular branch or tag:

```
git fetch origin <branch-name>
```

By specifying the branch, Git fetches updates only for the specified branch rather than all branches from the remote.

Fetch Output Analysis: After fetching, it is essential to analyze the output provided by Git. Here's an example of what might be displayed:

```
remote: Counting objects: 12, done.
remote: Compressing objects: 100% (8/8), done.
remote: Total 12 (delta 4), reused 10 (delta 2)
Unpacking objects: 100% (12/12), done.
From https://github.com/user/repo
 * [new branch]      feature     -> origin/feature
 * [new tag]         v1.2        -> v1.2
```

This output shows the progress of the fetch, including objects counted, compressed, and unpacked. It also indicates new branches and tags fetched from the remote.

By incorporating fetching into your workflow, you maintain up-to-date local references of remote branches which are crucial for coordinating collaborative development efforts.

5.5 Pushing to a Remote Repository

Pushing is one of the fundamental Git operations that allows you to transfer commits from your local repository to a remote repository. This process is essential for sharing progress, making collaborative workflows possible, and ensuring that project updates are synchronized among all contributors.

To perform a push operation, you utilize the git push command. This command is executed from the command line and requires specifying the remote repository and the branch you intend to push to. The general syntax for the git push command is as follows:

```
git push <remote> <branch>
```

Here, <remote> is the name of the remote repository, which is commonly origin—the default name assigned when you clone a repository. The <branch> represents the branch name you wish to push. For instance, if you are working on the main branch and your remote is origin, the command you would use is:

```
git push origin main
```

- **1. Basic Push Operation**

  Assuming that you have a branch named feature-branch and you want to push it to the remote repository named origin, the command would look like this:

  ```
  git push origin feature-branch
  ```

  Executing this command will upload all the commits from your feature-branch to the corresponding branch in the origin remote repository.

- **2. The –set-upstream Option**

  When pushing a branch for the first time, it is often useful to set the upstream reference, which establishes a tracking relationship between your local branch and the remote branch. The –set-upstream option (or its shorthand -u) accomplishes this. For example:

```
git push --set-upstream origin feature-branch
```

By setting the upstream, future git push and git pull commands can omit specifying the remote and branch name, simplifying the workflow.

- **3. Force Pushing**

  Under certain circumstances, such as when rewriting history or after a rebase, you may need to force push your changes. Force pushing is performed using the –force (or -f) option. Caution is advised as this can overwrite changes in the remote repository, potentially causing data loss for other collaborators:

  ```
  git push --force origin feature-branch
  ```

- **4. Using Refspecs for Push**

  Refspecs allow more granular control over what is pushed to the remote repository. Refspecs can specify different branches or tags. For example, pushing feature-branch to main in the remote repository can be achieved as follows:

  ```
  git push origin feature-branch:main
  ```

  This command pushes your local feature-branch to the main branch in the origin remote repository.

- **5. Managing Push Permissions**

  Push permissions are controlled by the remote's hosting service. Most remote repository hosting services, such as GitHub, Bitbucket, and GitLab, require authentication. Trying to push without proper authentication will result in an error. A common setup involves using SSH keys or HTTPS authentication mechanisms. Here is an example interaction for a repository requiring HTTPS authentication:

  ```
  Username for 'https://github.com': your-username
  Password for 'https://your-username@github.com':
  ```

  Modern Git versions also support personal access tokens (PAT) for HTTPS authentication, providing enhanced security over traditional password usage.

- **6. Common Issues During Pushing**

  One frequent issue encountered during pushing is the presence of divergent commits between the local and remote branches:

  ```
  error: failed to push some refs to 'https://github.com/user/repo.git'
  hint: Updates were rejected because the remote contains work that you do
  hint: not have locally. This is usually caused by another repository pushing
  hint: to the same ref. You may want to first integrate the remote changes
  hint: (e.g., 'git pull ...') before pushing again.
  hint: See the 'Note about fast-forwards' in 'git push --help' for details.
  ```

  This error occurs when there are commits in the remote branch that are not present in your local branch, generally due to updates by other collaborators. Resolving this involves pulling the latest changes from the remote repository and reconciling differences before attempting to push again:

  ```
  git pull origin feature-branch
  ```

Concluding this section, understanding and utilizing the git push command and its various options is vital for effective collaboration in Git. Mastery of pushing ensures that your contributions are consistently integrated with the team's shared repository.

5.6 Pulling from a Remote Repository

Pulling from a remote repository in Git is an essential operation that allows a user to fetch and integrate changes from a remote repository into the local repository. This operation combines two processes: fetching and merging. Fetching retrieves the latest changes from the remote repository without modifying the local working directory, while merging incorporates those fetched changes into the current branch.

To perform a pull operation, the git pull command is used. The syntax for this command is as follows:

```
git pull [options] [<repository> [<refspec>...]]
```

By default, git pull operates on the currently checked-out branch, resolving any changes by merging them into the branch. If no specific <repository> and <refspec> are given, Git assumes the configured upstream branch.

Let us break down the key elements and steps involved in the pull process in more detail:

Step 1: Fetching Changes

The first part of a pull operation involves fetching the changes from the remote repository. This is equivalent to executing the git fetch command. The git fetch command downloads objects and refs from another repository, specified by <repository>:

```
git fetch <repository>
```

If the repository argument is omitted, Git will use the default remote repository configured for the current branch, which is typically origin. For example:

```
git fetch origin
```

On successful completion, git fetch will have brought all the latest commits, files, and refs from the remote repository, updating the remote-tracking branches such as origin/main.

Output:

```
From https://github.com/user/repo
 * [new branch]      main       -> origin/main
```

Step 2: Merging Changes

After fetching, the next part of the pull operation merges these changes into the current branch in the local repository. The merge process integrates the newly fetched commits into the current branch. The operation performed is similar to running the following command:

```
git merge FETCH_HEAD
```

FETCH_HEAD is a reference to the state of the remote branch after the fetch operation. During the merge, Git will try to combine the changes received from the remote repository with the changes in the local repository. If there are no conflicts, the merge completes successfully. If conflicts are encountered, Git will prompt the user to resolve them manually.

Example: Performing a Pull Operation

Assuming the user is working on the main branch and wants to pull the latest changes from the origin remote, the command used will be:

```
git pull origin main
```

After execution, the following messages indicate successful fetching and merging:

Output:

```
remote: Enumerating objects: 5, done.
remote: Counting objects: 100% (5/5), done.
remote: Compressing objects: 100% (3/3), done.
remote: Total 3 (delta 2), reused 0 (delta 0), pack-reused 0
Unpacking objects: 100% (3/3), 2.34 KiB | 1.17 MiB/s, done.
From https://github.com/user/repo
 * branch            main       -> FETCH_HEAD
   3f3a78e..a1b2c3d  main       -> origin/main
Merge made by the 'recursive' strategy.
 file1.txt | 4 ++--
 1 file changed, 2 insertions(+), 2 deletions(-)
```

In this example, the output shows objects being counted, compressed, and unpacked during the fetch. Next, the branch main from the remote repository (origin) is merged into the local branch, using the recursive strategy, indicating the successful integration of changes.

Handling Merge Conflicts

If conflicts arise during the merge stage of a pull operation, Git will notify the user and mark the conflicted files. The user must manually resolve these conflicts before the merge can be finalized. For instance:

Example: Merge Conflict During Pull

```
Auto-merging file2.txt
CONFLICT (content): Merge conflict in file2.txt
Automatic merge failed; fix conflicts and then commit the result.
```

To resolve the conflict:

- Open the conflicted file(s) and reconcile the differences.
- Stage the resolved files using `git add <file>`.
- Complete the merge by committing the changes:

```
git commit
```

When conflicts have been resolved, and the commit is made, the pull process is complete, and the local repository is synchronized with the remote's state.

Pull with Rebase

An alternative to the merge-based pull is to rebase changes instead of merging them. This can be achieved with:

```
git pull --rebase
```

This command rebases the local commits on top of the fetched commits from the remote branch, resulting in a cleaner commit history, as it avoids unnecessary merge commits.

Understanding the intricacies of the `git pull` command and the processes of fetching and merging ensures efficient collaboration and synchronization with remote repositories. Whether merging or rebasing, mastering these operations is crucial for maintaining consistency and coherence across distributed projects.

5.7 Cloning Remote Repositories

Cloning a remote repository is a fundamental operation in Git that allows users to create a local copy of an existing remote repository. This process not only duplicates the repository's latest state but also includes its history and configurations, enabling effective collaboration and offline development.

The command `git clone` is used for this purpose. The general syntax of the command is as follows:

```
git clone <repository_url> [<directory_name>]
```

Here, `<repository_url>` specifies the URL of the remote repository to be cloned, and `[<directory_name>]` is an optional parameter that determines the name of the directory into which the repository will be cloned. If the directory name is omitted, Git will create a directory named after the repository itself.

Consider the following example where we clone a repository from a GitHub URL:

```
git clone https://github.com/username/repository.git
```

By executing this command, Git will:

- Create a directory named `repository`.
- Initialize a new Git repository within this directory.
- Set up the original repository as a remote named `origin`.
- Fetch all the branches and tags from the remote repository.
- Check out the default branch (usually `main` or `master`).

A similar invocation with a specified directory name looks like this:

```
git clone https://github.com/username/repository.git mydirectory
```

Executing this will clone the repository into a directory named mydirectory.

Upon successful cloning, the output will be as follows:

```
Cloning into 'repository'...
remote: Enumerating objects: 10, done.
remote: Counting objects: 100% (10/10), done.
remote: Compressing objects: 100% (5/5), done.
remote: Total 10 (delta 3), reused 10 (delta 3), pack-reused 0
Receiving objects: 100% (10/10), done.
Resolving deltas: 100% (3/3), done.
```

This indicates that all objects and references have been successfully copied and set up in the specified directory.

The git clone command also supports various options, which can be utilized to customize the cloning process. Some useful options include:

- -b <branch> or –branch <branch>: Clone a specific branch instead of the default branch.
- –single-branch: Create a single-branch clone, which excludes the history of other branches.
- –depth <depth>: Perform a shallow clone, fetching only the specified number of commits.

An example of cloning a specific branch:

```
git clone --branch develop https://github.com/username/repository.git
```

A shallow clone fetching only the latest 10 commits:

```
git clone --depth 10 https://github.com/username/repository.git
```

These options enable developers to tailor cloning according to their needs, potentially improving performance and saving bandwidth by limiting the amount of data transferred.

Post-cloning, the repository can be managed like any other Git repository. For instance, running git remote -v will list the remote URLs configured for the repository, usually showing the following:

```
origin https://github.com/username/repository.git (fetch)
origin https://github.com/username/repository.git (push)
```

This indicates that the remote origin is set up for both fetching and pushing. Additionally, users might want to verify the default branch checked out:

```
git branch
```

This will show a list of branches with the default branch prefixed by an asterisk (*).

To summarize, mastering the git clone command and its options is crucial for establishing a productive workflow with Git, enabling users to quickly and efficiently set up their local environment based on existing remote repositories.

5.8 Forking and Upstream Repositories

Forking a repository is a common practice in collaborative development, particularly in open-source projects. Forking creates a personal copy of another user's repository that resides in your Git hosting service account, such as GitHub, GitLab, or Bitbucket. This allows you to freely experiment and make changes in a sandboxed environment without affecting the original project. Understanding how forking works simultaneously with upstream repositories is essential for managing contributions and integrating changes efficiently.

To fork a repository, navigate to the desired repository on the hosting service and click on the "Fork" button. This action creates a new repository in your account that is a copy of the original. Consider the repository you forked as the **upstream repository**, and your fork as the **origin** repository.

In order to synchronize your fork with the upstream repository, it is crucial to configure your local Git repository to recognize the upstream repository. This involves setting a new remote reference to the upstream repository.

```
$ git remote add upstream https://github.com/original_owner/repository.git
```

With the upstream remote configured, you can fetch updates:

```
$ git fetch upstream
```

Once changes are fetched, you need to merge them into your local repository. Typically, you would merge these changes into your local 'main' branch, but it can be any branch upon which you want your work to be based.

```
$ git checkout main
$ git merge upstream/main
```

In cases where your local branches have diverged significantly from the upstream branch, rebasing instead of merging might be appropriate. Rebasing integrates changes from the upstream branch by replaying your local commits on top of the upstream commits.

```
$ git checkout main
$ git rebase upstream/main
```

After synchronizing your local repository with the upstream, you can push these updates to your forked repository on the hosting service.

```
$ git push origin main
```

This workflow enables continuous integration of changes from the upstream repository into your fork and facilitates the contribution of your changes back to the upstream project. When you have changes that you wish to contribute back to the upstream repository, you typically do so through a pull request (PR). This process involves:

- Ensuring your fork is up-to-date with the upstream main branch.
- Creating a feature branch from the 'main' branch for your changes.
- Pushing your feature branch to your fork and creating a PR from your feature branch to the upstream 'main'.

Creating a feature branch:

```
$ git checkout -b feature-branch
```

Make your changes and commit them to the feature branch.

```
$ git add .
$ git commit -m "Description of changes made"
```

Push the feature branch to your fork:

```
$ git push origin feature-branch
```

Then, navigate to the forked repository on the hosting service and create a PR. The hosting service interface typically guides you through the process, where you select the feature branch as the source and the upstream repository and branch as the destination.

By managing the forked repository and leveraging upstream synchronization effectively, you enable a seamless workflow that maximizes collaboration and minimizes integration conflicts in distributed projects. The ability to maintain alignment with the upstream repository while contributing back significant changes is pivotal in the open-source ecosystem and distributed development environments.

5.9 Managing Multiple Remotes

In a Git repository, it is possible to configure multiple remote repositories. This capability allows for more sophisticated workflows, such as working with both an internal corporate repository and a remote repository on a service like GitHub. Managing multiple remotes can streamline collaboration among various teams and foster more complex development paradigms.

To begin managing multiple remotes, one must understand the fundamental operations required to add, modify, and track these remote repositories. The following commands and configurations play a crucial role in this process.

To add a new remote repository, the `git remote add` command is used. The command syntax is straightforward:

```
git remote add <name> <url>
```

For example, to add a remote repository named `origin` that points to a GitHub repository, the command would be:

```
git remote add origin https://github.com/user/repository.git
```

Once added, you can verify the remotes associated with your repository using the `git remote` command, which lists all configured remotes:

```
git remote
```

The output might look like this:

```
origin
```

The `git remote show` command provides more detailed information about a specific remote:

```
git remote show origin
```

The output includes details on remote branches, whether they are tracked locally, and the default branch for push:

```
* remote origin
  Fetch URL: https://github.com/user/repository.git
  Push  URL: https://github.com/user/repository.git
  HEAD branch: main
  Remote branches:
    main                    tracked
  Local refs configured for 'git push':
    main                    pushes to main  (up to date)
```

Suppose you need to add another remote repository. You can do so simply by repeating the git remote add command with a different remote name and URL. For instance:

```
git remote add upstream https://github.com/another_user/another_repository.git
```

Afterward, using the git remote command will list both remotes:

```
origin
upstream
```

It is essential to correctly manage these remotes, especially when pushing changes to distinct repositories or fetching updates. If you want to push changes to a specific remote, you must specify the remote name in your git push command:

```
git push origin main
```

Or, to push to the newly added upstream remote:

```
git push upstream main
```

Fetching from a specific remote also requires indicating the remote name:

```
git fetch upstream
```

Sometimes, it becomes necessary to change the URL of an existing remote repository. This can be achieved with the git remote set-url command:

```
git remote set-url origin https://github.com/new_user/new_repository.git
```

Similarly, you can rename a remote for better clarity and organization:

```
git remote rename upstream p2p_remote
```

Removing a remote that is no longer needed is done with the git remote remove command:

```
git remote remove p2p_remote
```

The interplay between multiple remotes becomes particularly beneficial when working with forks and upstream repositories (as detailed in another section of this chapter). Configuring an upstream remote ensures that you can fetch updates from the original repository while keeping your forked repository up-to-date and synchronized.

Through these various commands and diligent management of multiple remotes, one can harness the power of distributed development flows more effectively. Understanding and utilizing the capabilities of multiple remote repositories significantly enhances collaborative work and development efficiency.

5.10 Understanding Remote Branches

Understanding remote branches in Git is crucial for effective collaboration within distributed version control systems. Remote branches are references to the state of branches in remote repositories. They act as bookmarks, telling Git where the branches in the remote repository were the last time you connected to it.

In Git, remote branches follow a specific naming convention to differentiate them from local branches. For example, if you have a remote named 'origin', and it has a branch called 'main', the remote branch will appear locally as 'origin/main'.

- Tracking branches help you stay in sync with remote branches. They are local branches that have a direct relationship to a remote branch. When you push or pull with these tracking branches, Git knows the exact location of the corresponding branch on the remote repository. To create a tracking branch, you typically use the '–track' option with the 'git checkout' command:

```
git checkout --track origin/main
```

This command sets up a local branch named 'main' that tracks the 'main' branch from the 'origin' remote. Now, commands like 'git pull' and 'git push' will automatically interact with 'origin/main'.

- You can list all available remote branches using the 'git branch' command with the '-r' flag, which stands for remote. The output will list all the remote branches that are currently known to your repository.

```
git branch -r
```

The output will resemble:

```
origin/HEAD -> origin/main
origin/develop
origin/feature-branch
origin/main
```

The 'origin/HEAD' reference shows which branch is the default branch for the remote repository. The remaining entries represent the remote branches available from the 'origin' remote repository.

To get detailed information about any specific remote branch, you can use the 'git show-branch' command:

```
git show-branch remotes/origin/main
```

This command provides a more detailed log of the commits and changes associated with 'origin/main'.

- Fetching remote branches involves downloading the changes from the remote repository and updating your remote branches to reflect these changes. The 'git fetch' command is used to update your remote-tracking branches:

```
git fetch origin
```

After fetching, your local state of the remote branches will be up-to-date with the remote repository. To see the changes fetched, you can use 'git log':

```
git log origin/main
```

This will show the commit history of 'origin/main', reflecting the latest updates from the remote repository.

- You can work with remote branches by checking them out, which creates a local branch associated with the remote branch. Use the following command to check out a remote branch:

```
git checkout -b feature-branch origin/feature-branch
```

This command creates a new local branch called 'feature-branch' and sets it to track 'origin/feature-branch'. You can now make changes on 'feature-branch' and push them back to 'origin/feature-branch':

```
git push origin feature-branch
```

To delete a remote branch, you use the 'git push' command with the '–delete' option:

```
git push origin --delete feature-branch
```

This removes the 'feature-branch' from the 'origin' remote repository.

- Upstream and downstream terminology is often used in the context of remote branches to describe the direction of data flow. An upstream branch is the primary source branch from which a local branch was derived or is synchronized. When a local branch has an upstream branch set, commands like 'git pull' and 'git push' can interact with it automatically. You can set an upstream branch using:

```
git branch --set-upstream-to=origin/main
```

This command sets the current branch to track 'origin/main' as its upstream branch.

- Refspecs are mapping instructions for Git, specifying how references (such as branches) on the remote side map to references on the local side. They are commonly used to selectively fetch or push specific branches. For example:

```
git fetch origin refs/heads/main:refs/remotes/origin/main
```

In this command, 'refs/heads/main' specifies the remote reference (branch) to fetch, and 'refs/remotes/origin/main' specifies the local reference to store the fetched branch.

Understanding and utilizing remote branches efficiently can significantly enhance your workflow, particularly when collaborating on shared projects.

Chapter 6

Collaboration Workflows

This chapter examines various collaborative development workflows in Git, including the forking workflow, feature branch workflow, and GitFlow workflow. It explains the process of handling pull requests and performing code reviews. The chapter also addresses the resolution of merge conflicts in team settings and the usage of rebasing in a collaborative environment. Additionally, it covers collaborating with submodules, integrating continuous integration and deployment (CI/CD), and outlines best practices to ensure effective teamwork.

6.1 Introduction to Collaborative Development

Collaborative development is a cornerstone of modern software engineering, enabling multiple developers to work on a codebase simultaneously. The advent of distributed version control systems (DVCS) like Git has revolutionized collaboration by providing tools and workflows that facilitate efficient and concurrent development. This section delves into the fundamental aspects of collaborative development using Git, laying the foundation for more advanced workflows discussed in subsequent sections.

Central to collaborative development is the concept of the repository, a storage space where the project's code and history are maintained. In

Git, repositories can be centralized or distributed, with each developer possessing a full copy of the repository, including its entire history. This decentralization enhances both offline access and redundancy.

An effective collaborative development environment requires a clear understanding of several key Git operations and concepts:

- **Distributed Version Control:** Unlike centralized version control systems, DVCS allows every contributor to have a full-fledged local repository with complete history tracking capabilities. This decentralization facilitates ease of branching, merging, and offline work.
- **Branching and Merging:** Branching allows developers to diverge from the main codebase to develop features or fixes in isolation. Merging is the process of integrating these branches back into the main codebase. Effective branching strategies are crucial for maintaining code stability and consistency.
- **Commits:** Each commit captures the state of the codebase at a particular point in time. Commits should be meaningful and atomic, encapsulating a single logical change. This practice aids in maintaining a clear project history.
- **Remote Repositories:** These serve as the reference points for collaboration, often hosted on platforms such as GitHub or GitLab. Push and pull operations synchronize local repositories with remote ones.
- **Pull Requests/ Merge Requests:** These facilitate code reviews and discussions before changes are merged into the main branch. They help maintain code quality and share knowledge among team members.

Consider an exemplary scenario where multiple developers are collaborating on a software project. Each developer clones the central repository to their local machine:

```
git clone https://github.com/user/repo.git
```

Developers can create branches to work on isolated features or fixes:

```
git checkout -b feature-branch
```

Once work on the feature is completed, the changes are committed locally:

```
git add .
git commit -m "Implemented new feature"
```

The developer then pushes their branch to the remote repository:

```
git push origin feature-branch
```

A pull request or merge request is created on the hosting platform, initiating a code review process. Other team members review the proposed changes, suggest modifications, and discuss the implementation. After approval, the feature branch is merged into the main branch, often following a rebase to maintain a linear commit history.

Program source code reviews are critical for ensuring code quality and fostering shared understanding among team members. Here's an example of how a team's review process might look in code comments:

```
Reviewer: "This function uses a deprecated API. Please update to use the new method."
Developer: "Updated as requested. Please review the latest commit."
```

Merge conflicts may arise during the collaborative process when changes from different branches cannot be automatically reconciled. These require manual resolution:

```
git pull origin main
# Resolve conflicts in the affected files
git add .
git commit -m "Resolved merge conflicts"
```

Rebasing is another critical aspect of collaborative development, especially when maintaining a clean project history. It can be used to apply local commits on top of the latest changes from the main branch:

```
git fetch origin
git rebase origin/main
```

If conflicts occur during rebase, they must be resolved, and the process continued:

```
git add .
git rebase --continue
```

To ensure robust and effective collaborative development, teams must adopt best practices such as regular communication, code reviews, continuous integration, and maintaining a clear branching model. The subsequent sections will explore specific workflows and strategies that enhance collaboration, enabling teams to maximize their productivity and code quality.

6.2 Forking Workflow

The forking workflow is an essential methodology in collaborative Git development, particularly well-suited for open source projects and situations where contributors do not have direct write access to the primary repository. This workflow leverages Git's decentralized nature, allowing developers to work independently on their copies of the repository while facilitating a streamlined integration process.

In the forking workflow, each contributor forks the official repository, creating their own copy of it within their personal namespace on the same Git hosting service (e.g., GitHub, GitLab). This process can be executed straightforwardly through the web interface of the hosting service by clicking a "Fork" button. Forking creates a duplicate repository under the user's account while preserving the full commit history and structure of the original project.

Once the repository has been forked, the contributor will clone it to their local development environment, initiating the typical Git workflow of making changes, committing, and pushing to their forked repository. The commands for these steps are as follows:

```
# Clone the forked repository to local
git clone https://github.com/username/forked-repo.git

# Navigate to the repository directory
cd forked-repo

# Create a new branch for the feature or bug fix
git checkout -b my-feature-branch
```

To ensure their fork remains up-to-date with the original repository, the contributor adds the original repository as a remote, often named 'upstream':

```
# Add the original repository as a remote named 'upstream'
git remote add upstream https://github.com/original-owner/original-repo.git
```

Periodically, the contributor fetches changes from the upstream repository and merges them into their fork to stay synchronized with ongoing developments:

```
# Fetch changes from the upstream repository
git fetch upstream

# Merge changes into the local main branch
git checkout main
git merge upstream/main
```

By following these steps, the contributor can integrate enhancements and updates from the primary repository, mitigating the risk of significant divergences between their fork and the official project.

When a feature or fix is complete, the contributor pushes their changes to a dedicated branch on their forked repository:

```
# Push changes to the feature branch on the forked repository
git push origin my-feature-branch
```

The next critical step is to initiate a pull request (PR) from the forked repository to the original repository. This process involves creating a merge request through the Git hosting service's web interface, specifying the source branch (e.g., 'my-feature-branch' in the forked repository) and the target branch in the original repository (e.g., 'main').

In the pull request description, the contributor should provide a concise yet comprehensive overview of the changes, potential impacts, and any related issues or enhancements. Good practices include linking to relevant issue trackers, incorporating detailed commit messages, and adding documentation where appropriate.

Once submitted, the pull request undergoes code review by the maintainers of the original repository. This review process often involves discussions, requests for changes, and running automated tests as part of Continuous Integration (CI) workflows. Reviewers assess the quality of the code, ensure adherence to project standards, and verify compatibility with the existing codebase.

Should the reviewers suggest changes, the contributor makes the necessary adjustments within the same branch and updates the pull request. The commit history should remain clean, and interactive rebasing can help tidy up the commit sequence:

```
# Make changes to the feature branch
git checkout my-feature-branch

# Commit changes
git commit -am "Incorporate feedback from code review"

# Rebase interactively to clean up commit history
git rebase -i main

# Push changes to the forked repository
# If rebased, force-push is required
git push --force origin my-feature-branch
```

After the pull request meets all requirements and passes review, it is merged into the original repository's target branch. The maintainer performing the merge has the discretion to use a merge commit, squash and merge, or rebase and merge, depending on the preferred workflow of the project.

Upon successful integration, the contributor may delete their feature branch from both their local and remote repositories to maintain a clean and manageable workspace:

```
# Delete the local feature branch
git branch -d my-feature-branch

# Delete the remote feature branch from the forked repository
git push origin --delete my-feature-branch
```

The forking workflow provides multiple benefits:

- Isolation: Contributors work independently on their forks, preventing disruptions to the main codebase.
- Security: Maintainers control write access and review changes before merging.
- Flexibility: Contributors can experiment and make broad changes without affecting others.
- Community Involvement: Lower barrier for external contributors to propose changes and improvements.

While effective, the forking workflow requires diligent synchronization with the upstream repository and a responsive code review process. Enhanced collaboration and communication practices ensure that contributions are welcomed, reviewed, and integrated smoothly, facilitating ongoing project development and improvement.

6.3 Feature Branch Workflow

The feature branch workflow is a popular branching strategy in Git used to facilitate parallel development and streamline the integration of new features. This workflow involves creating a dedicated branch for each feature or bug fix, ensuring that the main branch remains in a deployable state. By isolating development in branches, developers can work on features independently and mitigate risks associated with integration.

When adopting a feature branch workflow, the primary steps involve creating a branch for the new feature, making and committing changes, pushing the branch to the remote repository, and finally merging the feature branch back into the main branch. Below, we delve into each step with detailed instructions and best practices.

The initial step of the feature branch workflow is to ensure that the local repository is updated to reflect the latest changes from the remote repository. This can be achieved by performing a pull operation on the main branch.

```
git checkout main
git pull origin main
```

Next, create a new branch for the feature you plan to develop. It is crucial to choose a descriptive name for the branch that clearly indicates the purpose or scope of the feature.

```
git checkout -b feature/new-feature
```

The 'checkout -b' command creates a new branch named 'feature/new-feature' and checks it out so that any subsequent commits apply to this branch.

With the new feature branch ready, developers can proceed to implement the feature. This involves modifying, adding, or deleting files as necessary. Well-documented and frequent commits help maintain a clear development history, simplifying code reviews and future debugging. Commit changes with descriptive messages summarizing the purpose and content of each commit.

```
git add .
git commit -m "Implement initial version of the new feature"
```

After completing the changes, it is advisable to push the feature branch to the remote repository to ensure that code is backed up and available for other team members.

```
git push origin feature/new-feature
```

After pushing the branch, the next step is to create a pull request (PR) or merge request. This signals that the feature is ready for review and potential integration into the main branch. Platforms like GitHub and GitLab provide interfaces for creating and managing pull requests, which facilitate code reviews and discussions.

A critical aspect of the feature branch workflow is peer review. Code reviews help identify potential issues, ensure adherence to coding standards, and improve overall code quality. During the review process, reviewers may request changes or provide feedback. Developers should address these comments promptly, possibly making additional commits to refine the feature.

Once the pull request is approved, merge the feature branch into the main branch. It is often beneficial to rebase the feature branch onto the latest main branch before merging. Rebasing helps maintain a linear history and incorporates the latest changes from the main branch.

```
git fetch origin
git rebase origin/main
```

To resolve any conflicts that arise during the rebase, refer to the conflict markers in the affected files, edit the content to reconcile differences, and stage the resolved files.

Finally, perform the merge operation. On platforms like GitHub, this can typically be done directly through the web interface. If merging locally, switch to the 'main' branch and merge the feature branch:

```
git checkout main
git merge feature/new-feature
```

Once the feature is successfully integrated into the main branch, delete the feature branch to tidy up the repository.

```
git branch -d feature/new-feature
git push origin --delete feature/new-feature
```

Adopting a feature branch workflow has several advantages:

- It allows simultaneous development without affecting the main branch.
- It facilitates focused reviews.
- It maintains a clean and organized project history.

However, it requires rigorous discipline in managing branches and collaboration among team members to prevent issues such as long-lived feature branches and integration challenges.

6.4 GitFlow Workflow

The GitFlow Workflow is a robust branching model developed by Vincent Driessen that accommodates the need for continuous integration and release management strategies in software development. It offers a well-structured process suitable for managing large projects, multiple collaborators, and complex release schedules.

GitFlow employs a set of well-defined branches to facilitate parallel development and production-ready code deployment. Essential branches include: master, develop, feature, release, and hotfix. Each branch serves a distinct purpose and has specific rules governing its lifecycle.

The master branch always reflects a production-ready state. Every commit on the master branch must be deployable. The develop branch represents the latest development changes and integrates the work from various feature branches. When features are finished, they are merged into develop, preparing the environment for the next production release.

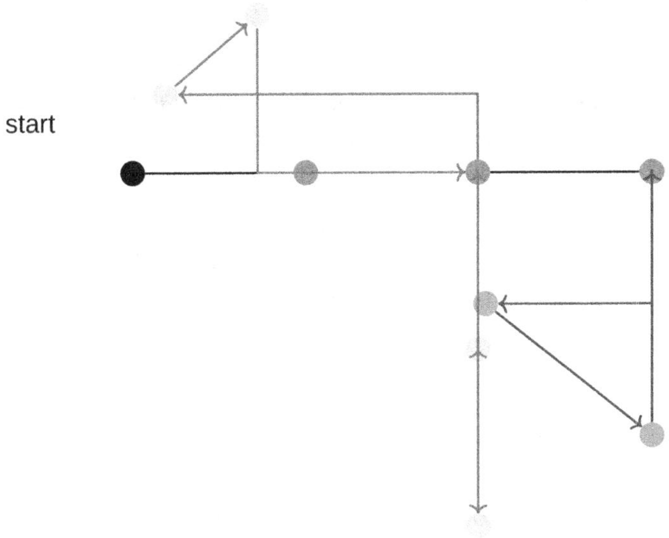

Figure 6.1: GitFlow Workflow branching model.

Feature branches are created off the develop branch and are dedicated to developing individual features. Once development on a feature is complete, it is merged back into develop, thereby integrating all changes.

```
$ git checkout develop
$ git checkout -b feature/feature-name
# develop the feature
$ git add .
$ git commit -m "Add feature-name"
```

```
$ git checkout develop
$ git merge feature/feature-name
$ git branch -d feature/feature-name
```

Release branches are created from the develop branch when a set of features is nearly ready for production release. These branches allow for last-minute bug fixes and minor improvements. Once the release is finalized, the branch is merged into both master and develop, ensuring all improvements are captured.

```
$ git checkout develop
$ git checkout -b release/v1.0.0
# final testing and fixes
$ git add .
$ git commit -m "Prepare release v1.0.0"
$ git checkout master
$ git merge release/v1.0.0
$ git tag -a v1.0.0 -m "Release version 1.0.0"
$ git checkout develop
$ git merge release/v1.0.0
$ git branch -d release/v1.0.0
```

Hotfix branches address urgent fixes that need to be applied directly to production. They are branched off master and merged into both master and develop after the fix is implemented to ensure the correction is included in future releases.

```
$ git checkout master
$ git checkout -b hotfix/bugfix-name
# apply the fix
$ git add .
$ git commit -m "Fix critical issue bugfix-name"
$ git checkout master
$ git merge hotfix/bugfix-name
$ git tag -a v1.0.1 -m "Hotfix release v1.0.1"
$ git checkout develop
$ git merge hotfix/bugfix-name
$ git branch -d hotfix/bugfix-name
```

By adhering to this model, GitFlow ensures that the code in the master branch is always stable and deployable, while allowing for continuous integration and regular releases through the effective use of branching. The system enables parallel development among multiple contributors, whereby features, bug fixes, and releases are managed systematically, reducing complexity and enhancing collaborative efficiency. This structured workflow is particularly advantageous for teams working on long-term projects where maintaining a stable release is critical amidst continuous development and integration efforts.

6.5 Pull Requests and Code Reviews

Pull requests (PRs) are integral components of collaborative workflows in Git, facilitating the formal process of proposing changes to a codebase. They allow contributors to notify team members about their changes, enabling discussions and reviews before the code is merged into the main repository. The effectiveness of pull requests is heightened through structured code reviews, which help maintain code quality and consistency.

Creating a Pull Request

To create a pull request, a contributor must first push their changes to a remote branch in the repository. This is commonly done from a feature branch, which isolates new development work. Here is an example of the workflow:

```
git checkout -b feature-branch
# Make changes and commit them
git commit -m "Implement new feature"
git push origin feature-branch
```

Once the changes are pushed to the remote repository, the contributor visits the repository's web interface (e.g., GitHub, GitLab, Bitbucket) to initiate a pull request. The essential steps include selecting the base branch (usually the main or master branch) and the compare branch (the feature branch). A detailed description of the changes and the rationale behind them should accompany the pull request.

Reviewing a Pull Request

When a pull request is opened, reviewers—who are often peers or senior developers—assess the changes. This review process includes:

- **Reading the Description**: Understanding the purpose and context of the changes.
- **Checking for Functionality**: Ensuring the code implements the intended functionality correctly.
- **Evaluating Code Quality**: Verifying adherence to coding standards and best practices, such as clear variable naming, modularity, and readability.
- **Testing**: Running automated tests and possibly manual tests to ensure that the new code does not introduce regressions or bugs.

- **Assessing Impact**: Considering how the changes affect the entire codebase, including potential interactions with other components and performance implications.

Reviewers may leave comments and request changes. Here is an example of fetching and reviewing a pull request locally:

```
# Assuming the PR is from a branch 'feature-branch' in 'user''s fork
git fetch origin pull/ID/head:feature-branch
git checkout feature-branch
# Inspect the changes
```

Review feedback is commonly communicated through inline comments on specific lines of code or through general comments on the pull request. If changes are requested, the contributor will make the necessary modifications and push updates to the feature branch, automatically updating the pull request.

Approval and Merging

Once the reviewers are satisfied with the changes, they approve the pull request. The next step is merging the changes into the base branch. Different merging strategies can be employed:

- **Merge Commit**: Combines all the commits from the feature branch into the base branch with a merge commit.

  ```
  git checkout main
  git merge feature-branch
  ```

- **Squash and Merge**: Combines all the commits into a single commit, resulting in a cleaner history.

  ```
  git checkout main
  git merge --squash feature-branch
  git commit -m "Feature implementation"
  ```

- **Rebase and Merge**: Rebases the feature branch onto the base branch, applying commits on top of the base history.

  ```
  git checkout main
  git rebase feature-branch
  ```

The choice of merging strategy depends on the team's workflow preferences and repository guidelines.

Best Practices for Pull Requests and Code Reviews

To optimize the pull request and code review process, consider the following best practices:

- **Small, Incremental Changes**: Smaller pull requests are easier to review and integrate. Large, monolithic changes can be overwhelming and more prone to errors.
- **Clear, Descriptive Commit Messages**: Each commit should clearly describe what changes were made and why, aiding reviewers in understanding the evolution of the feature.
- **Consistent Coding Standards**: Adherence to consistent coding styles and standards ensures readability and maintainability.
- **Automated Tests**: Implement automated tests for new features and ensure existing tests pass before submitting a pull request.
- **Timely Reviews**: Encourage timely reviews to maintain development momentum and avoid blocking other team members.
- **Respectful Feedback**: Provide constructive and respectful feedback, focusing on code improvements rather than personal criticism.

Using pull requests and code reviews as part of a collaborative development workflow not only enhances code quality but also fosters a culture of knowledge sharing and continuous improvement within the team.

6.6 Handling Merge Conflicts in Team Settings

Merge conflicts are a common occurrence in collaborative software development environments and resolving them efficiently is critical to maintaining team productivity. A merge conflict arises when two branches that are being merged have changes in the same part of a file or when one branch deletes a file that has been modified in the other. This section delves into strategies for identifying, resolving, and preventing merge conflicts in team settings.

Identifying Merge Conflicts:

When a merge conflict occurs, Git interrupts the merge process and flags the conflicting files. The output from Git will indicate which files have conflicts and provide markers within those files to highlight the nature of the conflict. Consider the following scenario where a conflict arises:

```
$ git merge feature-branch
Auto-merging example.txt
CONFLICT (content): Merge conflict in example.txt
Automatic merge failed; fix conflicts and then commit the result.
```

In the output above, Git specifies that the file example.txt has content conflicts. The conflicting sections in the file will be demarcated as follows:

```
<<<<<<< HEAD
This is content from the main branch.
=======
This is content from the feature branch.
>>>>>>> feature-branch
```

The text between «««< HEAD and ======= is from the current branch (e.g., main), while the text between ======= and »»»> feature-branch is from the branch being merged (e.g., feature-branch).

Resolving Merge Conflicts:

To resolve the conflict, one must edit the file to reconcile the differences. An effective way to manage this is through a three-way merge, which compares the common base version with the two conflicting versions. Tools such as kdiff3, meld, or Git's own git mergetool command can facilitate this process. After editing, remove the conflict markers and stage the resolved file:

```
$ git add example.txt
```

Once all conflicts have been resolved and staged, finalize the merge by committing the changes:

```
$ git commit
```

The commit message will often be pre-populated with details about the merge conflict resolution.

Strategies to Minimize Merge Conflicts:

Preventing merge conflicts from occurring in the first place is preferable and can be achieved through several best practices:

- **Frequent Pulls and Pushes**: Regularly pull changes from the remote repository and push local changes to keep branches up to date. This reduces the number of changes that must be reconciled during a merge.

```
$ git pull origin main
$ git push origin feature-branch
```

- **Feature Branch Workflow**: Isolate new development in feature branches that are short-lived. Merge each feature branch into the main branch once the feature is stable and complete.
- **Communication**: Maintain clear communication within the team about ongoing work to reduce the likelihood of simultaneous conflicting changes.
- **Code Reviews**: Implementing a stringent code review process can catch potential conflicts early. Reviewers can identify overlapping changes and coordinate accordingly.

Advanced Conflict Resolving Techniques:

In complex projects, merge conflicts may not be straightforward to resolve with basic three-way merging. In such cases, the following advanced techniques can be applied:

- **Interactive Rebase**: Rewriting commit history through interactive rebasing allows one to resolve conflicts incrementally. This can be particularly useful for addressing conflicts that span multiple commits.

```
$ git rebase -i HEAD~n
```

- **Conflict Resolution Tools**:
  - git rerere (Reuse Recorded Resolution): This command helps Git remember how you resolved conflicts and applies the same resolution to future conflicts in the same regions of the file.

```
$ git config --global rerere.enabled true
```

- **Cherry-Picking**: Selectively apply specific commits from one branch to another, which can help to isolate resolved sections before merging larger changes.

```
$ git cherry-pick <commit-hash>
```

These techniques, while more advanced, provide robust methods for effectively managing merge conflicts in multi-developer environments.

Understanding and applying these strategies for handling merge conflicts ensures smoother workflows and enhances overall team productivity. By utilizing both basic and advanced techniques, developers can efficiently resolve conflicts, facilitating cleaner integration of changes and maintaining codebase integrity.

6.7 Rebasing in a Collaborative Environment

Rebasing is a powerful feature in Git that allows developers to rewrite commit history in a linear fashion. This process is particularly useful in a collaborative environment to maintain a clean and understandable project history. However, it must be used with caution to avoid disrupting the shared repository. In this section, we will explore the purpose of rebasing, its advantages and disadvantages, and the best practices for its safe use within a team setting.

Purpose of Rebasing The primary goal of rebasing is to integrate changes from one branch into another by moving commits to a new base commit. This effectively ensures that the project history is linear, avoiding the complexities of a non-linear, branched history. By rebasing, developers can:

- Ensure a clean commit history.
- Facilitate bisecting commits for debugging purposes.
- Avoid merge commits that clutter the history.

How Rebasing Works Consider a scenario where a feature branch needs to be updated with changes from the main branch. Instead of merging the main branch into the feature branch, we can rebase the feature branch onto the main branch. The rebase process involves the following steps:

1. Identifying the common ancestor of the main and feature branches.
2. Creating temporary patches for each commit in the feature branch since the common ancestor.

3. Moving the feature branch pointer to the latest commit in the main branch.
4. Applying the patches sequentially onto the updated feature branch.

This sequence can be executed via the following command:

```
git checkout feature-branch
git rebase main
```

If there are conflicts during the rebase, Git will pause and allow the user to resolve them manually. After resolving the conflicts, use the following commands to continue the rebase:

```
git add <conflicted-files>
git rebase --continue
```

Advantages and Disadvantages Rebasing has several advantages that make it appealing for maintaining a clean project history:

- Linear History: Rebasing integrates changes without creating merge commits, resulting in a straight commit line.
- Simplified Conflicts: Resolving conflicts during a rebase can be more straightforward since each commit is applied individually.
- Cleaner Project History: The project's commit history is easier to read and understand, which is beneficial for both current and future developers.

However, rebasing also has its drawbacks:

- Complexity: Rebasing can be more complex than merging, especially for new users.
- Risk of Data Loss: Incorrect rebasing can potentially lose commits that are not properly managed.
- Rewriting History: In a shared repository, rebasing can interfere with other developers' work if not communicated properly.

Best Practices for Rebasing in a Team To leverage the benefits of rebasing while mitigating its risks, consider the following best practices in a collaborative environment:

- Rebase Before Pushing: Always rebase local changes before pushing to the shared repository, ensuring that your branch integrates smoothly with the latest upstream changes.
- Avoid Rebasing Shared History: Never rebase commits that have already been pushed to a shared repository, as this can cause confusion and overwrite others' work.
- Frequent Communication: Communicate with your team when performing rebases, especially if working on long-running branches.
- Use Interactive Rebase: The interactive rebase (`git rebase -i`) allows for more control, enabling you to reorder, squash, or edit commits as needed.

For example, an interactive rebase can be initiated with:

```
git rebase -i HEAD~n
```

Here, n represents the number of commits from HEAD that you wish to rebase interactively. This command will open an editor where you can specify actions for each commit.

Handling Rebase Conflicts Conflicts encountered during rebasing are similar to those during a merge. If a conflict arises, Git will stop at the problematic commit and mark the conflicting files. Resolve these conflicts by editing the files and then staging them:

```
git add <conflicted-file>
```

After resolving all conflicts, continue the rebase process with:

```
git rebase --continue
```

If further conflicts arise, repeat the process. To abort the rebase at any point, use:

```
git rebase --abort
```

Rebasing is a valuable tool for maintaining a streamlined commit history in collaborative development. By adhering to best practices, teams can integrate changes cleanly, preserve a linear project history, and enhance overall project manageability. Using rebasing properly requires a clear understanding of its mechanisms and diligent communication within the team to ensure smooth and error-free collaboration. When used appropriately, rebasing can significantly enhance the quality and navigability of a project's version history.

6.8 Collaborating with Submodules

Submodules in Git offer a mechanism to incorporate external repositories within your own. This functionality is particularly beneficial when dealing with projects that are structured in a modular fashion, or when you need to include third-party libraries that are managed independently. Utilizing submodules effectively can streamline collaboration across separate development teams or projects.

A submodule is essentially a repository nested inside another repository, where the nested repository maintains its own history and can be worked on independently of the parent repository.

To begin working with submodules, you must first understand how to add a submodule to your project. This is accomplished using the git submodule add command. Suppose you have a parent repository and you want to include a project named library-repo from GitHub. The command to achieve this would be:

```
git submodule add https://github.com/username/library-repo.git path/to/local-folder
```

This command will clone the library-repo inside the specified local folder and track it as a submodule. It is important to commit the changes to your parent repository to reflect this addition:

```
git add .gitmodules path/to/local-folder
git commit -m "Added submodule library-repo"
```

The .gitmodules file is a configuration file that stores the mapping between the submodule project URL and the local directory. It is automatically created when you add a submodule.

When you clone a repository containing submodules, the submodules are not automatically cloned. To clone a repository with all its submodules, use the –recurse-submodules option:

```
git clone --recurse-submodules https://github.com/username/parent-repo.git
```

Alternatively, if you have already cloned the repository and you need to initialize and fetch the submodules, execute:

```
git submodule init
git submodule update
```

When collaborating with submodules, you will routinely need to update them. If the submodule repository has new commits and you need to bring these changes into your parent project, navigate to the submodule directory and pull the changes:

```
cd path/to/local-folder
git pull origin main
cd ../
git add path/to/local-folder
git commit -m "Updated submodule library-repo"
```

Conflicts can arise when multiple collaborators update a submodule independently. Proper communication is crucial to manage these dependencies diligently. If a conflict does arise, you will need to manually merge the changes within the submodule and update the parent repository accordingly.

Removing a submodule involves several steps. First, delete the submodule entry from the .gitmodules file:

```
git submodule deinit -f -- path/to/local-folder
rm -rf .git/modules/path/to/local-folder
git rm -f path/to/local-folder
```

Then commit the changes to reflect the submodule removal:

```
git commit -m "Removed submodule library-repo"
```

When dealing with large-scale projects, it is common to use multiple submodules. Each submodule can evolve independently, making it essential to keep track of changes efficiently. Integrating Continuous Integration (CI) and Continuous Deployment (CD) workflows can automate this process to ensure that submodules are continuously validated and integrated into the parent project.

Careful management and consistent communication help maximize the benefits of using Git submodules, enhancing modularity and fostering more effective collaboration across diverse teams.

6.9 Continuous Integration and Deployment (CI/CD)

Continuous Integration and Deployment (CI/CD) is a set of practices in software development aiming to improve software delivery speed and quality. CI/CD automates the building, testing, and deployment processes, ensuring that the codebase remains in a deployable state and that integration issues are identified and addressed promptly.

Continuous Integration (CI) is the practice of merging all developers' working copies to a shared mainline several times a day. By integrating frequently, teams can detect issues early, which can be fixed more easily. The process involves automated testing to ensure that each integration is verified by creating a build and running a suite of tests. CI is instrumental in maintaining code quality and ensuring that the mainline remains healthy.

Continuous Deployment (CD), on the other hand, extends CI by automating the release of the integrated code to production whenever a change is detected. This practice ensures that new features and bug fixes are delivered to end-users as soon as they are ready.

Integration with Git

Integrating CI/CD with Git can significantly streamline the workflow for development teams. Git's branching and merging capabilities align well with CI/CD's goals of frequent integration and continuous delivery.

To integrate CI/CD with a Git repository, developers typically use CI/CD services like Jenkins, Travis CI, CircleCI, or GitHub Actions. These services monitor the Git repository for changes, automatically triggering the build and deployment processes when code is pushed or merged. Below is an example configuration for a CI service using GitHub Actions:

```
name: CI/CD Pipeline

on:
  push:
    branches:
      - main

jobs:
  build:
    runs-on: ubuntu-latest

    steps:
    - uses: actions/checkout@v2
      with:
```

```
          fetch-depth: 0

      - name: Set up Node.js
        uses: actions/setup-node@v2
        with:
          node-version: '14'

      - name: Install dependencies
        run: npm install

      - name: Run tests
        run: npm test

  deploy:
    runs-on: ubuntu-latest
    needs: build

    steps:
    - uses: actions/checkout@v2
      with:
        fetch-depth: 0

    - name: Deploy to production
      run: |
        echo "Deploying to production server"
        # Insert deployment commands here
```

In this example, GitHub Actions is used to define a CI/CD pipeline. The pipeline triggers on any push to the 'main' branch. It defines a job 'build' which involves checking out the repository, setting up the Node.js environment, installing dependencies, and running tests. If the 'build' job succeeds, the 'deploy' job is triggered to deploy the code to the production environment.

Pipeline Stages

A typical CI/CD pipeline consists of the following stages:

- **Source Stage**: Detects changes in the source code repository. Tools like GitHub Actions or Jenkins poll the repository to detect changes.
- **Build Stage**: Compiles the application's source code to create the executable or distributable version of the application. This stage ensures that the code compiles correctly and identifies issues early.
- **Test Stage**: Runs automated tests to validate the code's correctness. Tests can include unit tests, integration tests, and end-to-end tests. This stage ensures the code behaves as expected.
- **Deploy Stage**: Deploys the built and tested application to a production-like environment for final verification. This ensures

that the deployment process works correctly and the application functions in the deployment environment.

- **Release Stage**: Releases the application to the production environment. This stage involves additional smoke tests to validate that the deployment is successful and the application is running as expected.

Automated Testing Integration

Automated tests are central to the CI/CD pipeline. They ensure that changes do not break existing functionality. There are various types of tests that can be integrated into the pipeline:

- **Unit Tests**: Test individual units or components of the application. They are fast and run in isolation.
- **Integration Tests**: Test the interaction between different components or systems. These tests ensure that integrated components work together as expected.
- **End-to-End Tests**: Test the application from the user's perspective. They simulate user interactions and test the entire application flow.

Here's an example of how to run automated tests as part of the CI pipeline using GitHub Actions:

```
name: CI Pipeline

on:
  push:
    branches:
      - main

jobs:
  test:
    runs-on: ubuntu-latest

    steps:
    - uses: actions/checkout@v2
      with:
        fetch-depth: 0

    - name: Set up Node.js
      uses: actions/setup-node@v2
      with:
        node-version: '14'

    - name: Install dependencies
      run: npm install
```

```
    - name: Run unit tests
      run: npm test
```

Deployment Strategies

Deploying new code to production is a critical step in the CD process. There are several strategies to minimize the risk of deployment failures:

- **Blue-Green Deployment**: This strategy involves running two identical production environments, Blue and Green. At any time, only one environment serves live production traffic. When deploying a new version, it is deployed to the inactive environment. After thorough testing, the traffic is switched to the new environment.
- **Canary Deployment**: This method involves gradually rolling out the new version to a subset of users before deploying it to the entire user base. This approach allows for monitoring the new version's performance on a small scale and mitigating any issues before a full deployment.

```
#!/bin/bash

# Deploy to a subset of servers (canary)
for server in canary1.example.com canary2.example.com; do
  echo "Deploying to $server..."
  scp new_version.tar.gz user@$server:/path/to/deploy
  ssh user@$server 'cd /path/to/deploy && tar -xzf new_version.tar.gz && ./
      deploy_script.sh'
done

# Monitor canary servers and rollback if necessary
# Assuming monitoring script is available
if ./monitor_canary.sh; then
  echo "Canary deployment succeeded, deploying to remaining servers..."
  for server in server1.example.com server2.example.com; do
    echo "Deploying to $server..."
    scp new_version.tar.gz user@$server:/path/to/deploy
    ssh user@$server 'cd /path/to/deploy && tar -xzf new_version.tar.gz && ./
        deploy_script.sh'
  done
else
  echo "Canary deployment failed, rolling back..."
  # Rollback commands
fi
```

These strategies enable teams to deploy frequently and confidently, ensuring that new features and updates reach end-users safely and efficiently. Integrating CI/CD into the development workflow not only improves collaboration and productivity but also enhances software quality and user satisfaction.

6.10 Best Practices for Team Collaboration

Effective collaboration in Git requires adhering to a set of best practices that ensure smooth operation, high code quality, and maintainable project history. This section provides specific guidelines to enhance team collaboration in Git-based projects.

1. Consistent Naming Conventions: Enforcing naming conventions for branches, commits, and tags ensures that everyone on the team understands the purpose of each branch without ambiguity. Common conventions include:

- Prefixes for branch names such as feature/, bugfix/, release/.
- Descriptive, concise commit messages that follow a pattern, for example, <type>: <subject> where <type> might be feat, fix, docs, etc.
- Versioning tags formatted using Semantic Versioning, e.g., v1.0.0.

2. Code Reviews: Implementing a robust code review process strengthens code quality and knowledge sharing. Consider the following guidelines for code reviews:

- Use Pull Requests (PRs) to propose changes and facilitate discussions.
- Establish criteria for PR approval, such as requiring at least two reviewers or ensuring test case coverage.
- Provide constructive feedback, focusing on improvement rather than criticism.
- Encourage reviewers to test changes locally to verify functionality.

3. Small, Frequent Commits: Smaller commits with a single purpose are easier to review, test, and revert if necessary. To enforce this, team members should:

- Commit often, ideally after each significant change or logical unit of work.

- Squash trivial or fixup commits before merging to prevent clutter in the project history.

4. Branching Strategy: Develop and adhere to a branching strategy that suits the team's workflow. Common strategies include:

- Feature Branch Workflow: All feature development occurs in isolated branches derived from the main branch, promoting focused and parallel work.
- GitFlow: A more structured approach with multiple branch types, including develop, feature/, release/, and hotfix/, providing a clear release pipeline.
- Trunk-Based Development: Developers commit frequently to a shared trunk, supported with short-lived feature branches and extensive automated testing.

5. Automated Testing and CI/CD: Integrate Continuous Integration and Continuous Deployment (CI/CD) in the development pipeline to ensure that every change is tested. Key practices include:

- Use CI tools like Jenkins, Travis CI, or GitHub Actions to run automated tests on each push or PR.
- Ensure that the entire test suite passes before allowing merges into the main branch.
- Automate deployment processes to ensure consistency across environments, reducing the risk of human error.

6. Clear Documentation: Maintain comprehensive documentation for the project, including guidelines on setting up the local environment, contributing, and coding standards. Good practices include:

- Maintain a README.md file with an overview, setup instructions, and basic usage.
- Use a contribution guide (CONTRIBUTING.md) to outline the process for submitting changes, reporting bugs, and other contributions.
- Keep architecture and technical documentation up to date, ideally in a docs/ directory within the repository.

7. Conflict Resolution: Handle merge conflicts promptly with a consistent approach to minimize disruption. Recommended steps include:

- Regularly pull changes from the main branch to keep feature branches updated.
- Resolve conflicts locally and test thoroughly before pushing changes.
- Communicate with teammates when large-scale refactoring or complex merges are necessary to coordinate efforts.

8. Regular Synchronization: Encourage regular synchronization across the team to align on progress and address blockers:

- Schedule daily stand-ups or check-ins to discuss current tasks, progress, and impediments.
- Use project management tools like Jira, Trello, or GitHub Projects to track tasks and facilitate transparent workflow.

9. Respect and Collaboration: Foster a culture of mutual respect and open communication. Key elements include:

- Respect differing opinions and approaches to problem-solving.
- Encourage pair programming or mob programming sessions to promote collaboration and knowledge sharing.
- Celebrate team achievements and recognize individual contributions.

Implementing these best practices will enhance team efficiency, maintain high standards of code quality, and foster a collaborative and harmonious development environment.

Chapter 7

Advanced Git Techniques

This chapter explores advanced Git techniques, starting with rewriting history using Git rebase and interactive rebase. It covers methods for amending, squashing, and splitting commits, as well as utilizing the reflog to recover lost commits. The chapter also discusses using Git bisect for debugging, handling submodules and subtrees, and working with partial and shallow clones, providing in-depth insights into more sophisticated ways of managing and troubleshooting your Git repositories.

7.1 Introduction to Advanced Techniques

In this section, we delve into advanced Git techniques that transcend the basic commands and workflows covered in earlier chapters. These advanced methodologies are vital for developers seeking to streamline their version control processes, enhance collaboration efficiency, and maintain cleaner, more accurate repository histories. Building on the foundational knowledge of Git's distributed version control system, we will explore sophisticated operations such as rewriting commit history, debugging, leveraging submodules, and optimizing clone operations.

Git rebase is an integral part of advanced Git operations. It allows the modification of commit history in a linear fashion, making the repository history cleaner and more understandable. Rather than merging branches, which can introduce complex merge commits, rebasing rewrites the commit history by applying changes from one branch onto another as new commits. This method enables a more straightforward, chronological commit history that can be crucial for maintaining the clarity of a project's development timeline.

```
git checkout feature-branch
git rebase main
```

In the snippet above, changes from the 'feature-branch' are reapplied on top of the 'main' branch. This workflow ensures the feature branch is derived from the current state of the main branch, reducing potential conflicts when merging later on.

Interactive rebase elevates this technique by providing fine-grained control over each commit during the rebase process. By using the following command, you initiate an interactive rebase session:

```
git rebase -i HEAD~n
```

Here, 'n' denotes the number of commits from the current 'HEAD' to include in the rebase. The interactive mode opens an editor where you can choose to pick, reword, squash, or edit commits. This capability allows for meticulous adjustments, such as combining multiple commits into one (squashing) or modifying commit messages for clarity.

Another powerful aspect is the ability to amend commits. This operation is particularly useful when you need to correct or enhance the latest commit. By using:

```
git commit --amend
```

you can modify the most recent commit by altering its message or including additional changes. This command effectively overwrites the last commit with the new state, enabling corrections without creating unnecessary, separate commits.

Squashing commits reduces the clutter of multiple minor commits into a single, cohesive commit. This practice is especially beneficial when finalizing a feature branch before merging it into the main branch. During an interactive rebase, you can squash commits by replacing 'pick' with 'squash' for the desired commits, ensuring a cleaner project history.

Sometimes, it is necessary to split a large commit into multiple smaller commits. This practice can make reviewing changes more manageable and help isolate specific changes for reference or debugging purposes. To split commits, you would interrupt an interactive rebase session (by specifying 'edit' for the commit to split) and then utilize staging and the 'git commit' command to create smaller, logically distinct commits.

Recovering lost commits is another advanced technique, facilitated by the Git reflog. The reflog records updates to the 'HEAD' of a repository, providing a mechanism to retrieve commits that seem irretrievable. For instance, if a commit is accidentally discarded, it can be found and restored using:

```
git reflog
```

From the reflog, identify the commit's reference and perform a reset or checkout to recover it.

Using 'git bisect' for debugging is a methodical approach to pinpointing the exact commit that introduced a bug. By performing a binary search through the commit history, 'git bisect' narrows down the potential problematic commits efficiently, aiding in timely resolutions with minimal manual intervention.

Submodules and subtrees serve distinct purposes in managing dependencies on other Git repositories. Submodules link to external repositories within a parent repository, while subtrees integrate the content directly. These tools are indispensable when managing projects with dependencies that should remain in sync with external repositories.

Partial and shallow clones optimize repository clones by reducing the amount of data transferred and stored locally. Partial cloning fetches only specific subsets of a repository, while shallow cloning limits the clone depth, including just the most recent history. These techniques are especially useful for large repositories where full clones would be impractical.

These advanced techniques are vital for sophisticated project management, offering solutions to common challenges encountered in complex development environments. Embracing them not only enhances workflow efficiency but also ensures a robust and maintainable codebase.

7.2 Rewriting History with Git Rebase

Git Rebase is a powerful command that allows developers to rewrite the commit history of a branch. This command facilitates creating cleaner, more linear histories by moving or combining commits from one branch onto another. It is especially useful for crafting a series of commits that represent logical units of work, and it can simplify the history before merging it into the main branch.

Rebasing essentially combines all the changes from one branch and applies them to another. The primary difference from a merge operation is that rebase 'replays' the changes instead of merging the histories. This ensures the final branch history appears linear, without the additional merge commits.

To use the rebase command, navigate to the desired branch and execute the following command to start the rebase process:

```
git rebase <base-branch>
```

where <base-branch> is the branch you want to rebase onto. Git will then reapply each commit in your current branch on top of the <base-branch>.

For example, assume we have the following commit history:

```
  A---B---C---D feature
 /
E---F---G main
```

Executing the command git rebase main from the feature branch will replay the commits A, B, C, and D on top of the latest commit G in the main branch.

```
E---F---G---A'---B'---C'---D' feature
```

Each commit is effectively rewritten as a new commit (A', B', C', and D') on top of main's history. This results in a linear sequence without the divergences typically introduced by a merge commit.

Conflicts can arise if changes in the feature branch overlap or are incompatible with changes in the main branch. When a conflict happens, Git will pause the rebase process and prompt you to resolve these conflicts manually. The status of the rebase process can be checked using:

```
git status
```

After resolving each conflict, the rebase can be continued with:

```
git rebase --continue
```

If you need to abort the rebase process at any time and return to the state before the rebase attempt, execute:

```
git rebase --abort
```

It is important to note that rebasing changes commit IDs because it rewrites their history. This action can potentially rewrite history that has already been shared with others, leading to significant complications.

Therefore, it is considered good practice to perform rebases only on local changes that have not been pushed to a public or shared repository.

While straightforward rebasing replays all commits, interactive rebasing introduces additional flexibility, such as editing, reordering, and squashing commits into a single, cohesive unit. This form of rebase begins with the command:

```
git rebase -i <base-branch>
```

Interactive rebase then presents a list of commits for editing in the text editor defined by your Git settings. Each commit is presented with an action keyword (e.g., pick, reword, edit, squash). By manipulating these keywords and reordering lines, you can customize how the commit history is rewritten.

For example, initiating interactive rebase:

```
git rebase -i HEAD~4
```

This opens the text editor with the last four commits:

```
pick f7f3f6d Add feature X
pick 310154e Fix bug Y
pick a5f4a0d Improve performance
pick 4e7d18b Refactor module
```

By changing "pick" to "squash" on the third commit, we can combine "Improve performance" into the previous commit. The resultant editor view modifies as follows:

```
pick f7f3f6d Add feature X
pick 310154e Fix bug Y
squash a5f4a0d Improve performance
pick 4e7d18b Refactor module
```

After saving and closing the editor, Git will replay the commits, combining "Improve performance" with "Fix bug Y". This ability to customize the commit history is crucial for maintaining a clean, understandable project history, especially before integrating significant changes into shared repositories.

Rebasing is a fundamental concept in Git's toolkit for managing commit history, providing control over the repository's evolution and facilitating collaborative development. This section builds upon concepts previously introduced, enriching your understanding of Git rebase for more sophisticated repository management.

7.3 Interactive Rebase

Interactive rebase is a powerful Git feature that allows users to rewrite the commit history in a way that is cleaner, more logical, and easier to understand. When performed correctly, it can make the project's history much more readable and maintainable. The functionality of interactive rebase extends beyond simple history rewrites; it also includes actions like editing, reordering, squashing, and even dropping commits.

To start an interactive rebase, use the following command:

```
git rebase -i <base-commit>
```

Here, <base-commit> is the commit on top of which you want to rebase. Typically, this will be a commit hash or a branch reference.

When you issue the git rebase -i command, Git opens an editor displaying a list of commits in the range chosen for rebasing. Each line in the editor starts with a command (by default pick), followed by the commit hash and commit message. The default listing looks like this:

```
pick a1b2c3d Commit message one
pick e4f5g6h Commit message two
pick i7j8k9l Commit message three
```

Each pick command can be replaced with other commands during the interactive rebase:

- pick - Use the commit as-is.
- reword - Use the commit but edit the commit message.
- edit - Use the commit but stop for amending.
- squash - Combine this commit with the previous commit.
- fixup - Similar to squash, but discard the commit's log message.
- exec - Run a shell command.
- drop - Remove the commit.

Editing Commit Messages

Suppose you want to edit the commit message of Commit message two. Change pick to reword:

```
pick a1b2c3d Commit message one
reword e4f5g6h Commit message two
pick i7j8k9l Commit message three
```

When you save and close the editor, Git will open another editor where you can edit the commit message of Commit message two.

Squashing Commits

Squashing merges multiple commits into a single, cohesive commit. To squash Commit message two and Commit message three into one, change their commands to squash:

```
pick a1b2c3d Commit message one
pick e4f5g6h Commit message two
squash i7j8k9l Commit message three
```

After saving, the editor will open again, allowing you to merge and edit the commit messages of the squashed commits.

Reordering Commits

You can also change the order of commits by simply reordering the lines in the editor. For example, to move Commit message three before Commit message two:

```
pick a1b2c3d Commit message one
pick i7j8k9l Commit message three
pick e4f5g6h Commit message two
```

Dropping Commits

If a commit is no longer needed, the drop command can be used to remove it. If you decide to drop Commit message two, alter the file like so:

```
pick a1b2c3d Commit message one
drop e4f5g6h Commit message two
pick i7j8k9l Commit message three
```

Implementing Changes During Rebasing

The edit command pauses the rebase process, allowing changes to be made to a commit. Use this command if you notice an error in Commit message two's code:

```
pick a1b2c3d Commit message one
edit e4f5g6h Commit message two
pick i7j8k9l Commit message three
```

After saving, the rebase process stops at Commit message two. You can then edit this commit:

```
git commit --amend
```

Once changes are made, continue rebasing with:

```
git rebase --continue
```

Aborting a Rebase

If at any point the rebase must be aborted due to conflicts or errors, the following command restores the repository to its original state:

```
git rebase --abort
```

Understanding and leveraging interactive rebase can significantly refine the commit history, making it both compact and meaningful. This technique equips developers with the ability to curate a logical sequence of changes, enhancing the legibility and maintenance of the codebase.

7.4 Amending Commits

In Git, amending commits is a powerful technique that allows you to modify the most recent commit. This is particularly useful for correcting mistakes, adding forgotten changes, or improving commit messages. By amending commits, you can maintain a clean and concise project history. The primary command used to amend a commit is:

```
git commit --amend
```

This command opens a text editor where you can modify the commit message. However, its functionality extends beyond just changing messages. Let's delve into the specifics of amending commits.

To better understand amending commits, let's consider a scenario. Assume you have made a commit with the message "Initial commit" but later realized that you forgot to add a crucial file. First, stage the new file:

```
git add forgotten_file.txt
```

Next, run the commit amend command:

```
git commit --amend
```

You will be prompted with the previous commit message "Initial commit." At this point, you can change the commit message if desired. After saving and closing the text editor, the new file forgotten_file.txt is included in the amended commit.

Sometimes, you might only need to amend the commit message without changing the staged files. To do this, utilize the -no-edit flag:

```
git commit --amend --no-edit
```

This command retains the commit message from the previous commit while including any new changes staged in the index. If no new changes are staged, it only modifies the commit metadata, such as the commit message timestamp.

Consider a more complex scenario where you realize that the previous commit message is too vague. Suppose the commit message was "Fixes". To provide more context, use:

```
git commit --amend -m "Fix issue with user login feature"
```

This replaces the previous commit message "Fixes" with a more descriptive message without opening the text editor. The new message becomes "Fix issue with user login feature".

Amending commits impacts only the most recent commit. If you need to amend older commits, interactive rebase is more suitable (covered in another section).

While amending commits can be incredibly useful, it's important to recognize its limitations and precautions. Amending is a history-rewriting technique; therefore, changing commits that have already been shared with others can lead to collaboration issues. Rewriting shared history should be done with caution, communicating changes to your team to avoid disruption.

When working with remote repositories, and if the amended commit has already been pushed, you need to force push the amended commit:

```
git push --force
```

This force push updates the remote branch to match the amended commit. However, force-pushing can overwrite changes made by others, potentially causing data loss or conflicts. Always communicate with your team before performing force pushes on a shared branch.

To check the impact of an amended commit before pushing, use the `git log` command:

```
git log -1
```

This command shows the most recent commit, allowing you to verify that the amendments are as expected. Examining the commit metadata, such as author, date, and message, helps confirm that your changes have been correctly applied.

Amending commits also involves the concept of commit hashes. Each commit in Git is identified by a unique SHA-1 hash. When you amend a commit, its hash changes due to the modified content or metadata. Consequently, the commit becomes an entirely new commit, distinct from the original one. This is why careful consideration is necessary when amending commits, especially for shared repositories.

7.5 Squashing Commits

In Git, squashing commits is a powerful technique for combining multiple sequential commits into a single commit. This practice can be especially useful for creating a cleaner, more readable project history by condensing a series of small changes, bug fixes, or experimental commits into one comprehensive update. Squashing is often employed to tidy up commit history before merging a feature branch into the main branch.

To illustrate the squashing process, consider a feature branch with the following commit history:

```
commit a1b2c3d4: Added initial implementation of feature X
commit e5f6g7h8: Fixed minor bug in feature X
commit i9j0k1l2: Updated comments and documentation for feature X
```

To begin the squashing process, we use the git rebase command in interactive mode. Start by running the following command:

```
git rebase -i HEAD~3
```

This command initiates an interactive rebase of the last three commits on the current branch. The editor will open with a list of commits to be rebased, similar to the following:

```
pick a1b2c3d4 Added initial implementation of feature X
pick e5f6g7h8 Fixed minor bug in feature X
pick i9j0k1l2 Updated comments and documentation for feature X
```

In the interactive rebase list, each commit is prefixed with the command "pick" by default. To squash the second and third commits into the first commit, change the "pick" command for the second and third commits to "squash" (or the shorthand "s"). The modified list should look like this:

```
pick a1b2c3d4 Added initial implementation of feature X
squash e5f6g7h8 Fixed minor bug in feature X
squash i9j0k1l2 Updated comments and documentation for feature X
```

Save and close the file to proceed with the rebase. Git will then attempt to apply the commits with the specified squashing. If successful, another editor window will open, allowing you to edit the commit message of the squashed commit. This commit message will now include the messages of all squashed commits, providing the opportunity to combine them into a single coherent message:

```
# This is a combination of 3 commits.
# The first commit's message is:
Added initial implementation of feature X

# This is the 2nd commit message:
Fixed minor bug in feature X

# This is the 3rd commit message:
Updated comments and documentation for feature X
```

Edit the combined commit message to be concise and descriptive:

```
Added initial implementation of feature X with bug fixes and documentation updates
```

After saving the commit message, the rebase will complete, and the history for the branch will be rewritten as a single, consolidated commit:

```
commit a1b2c3d4 Added initial implementation of feature X with bug fixes and documentation updates
```

If conflicts arise during the rebase process, Git will pause the rebase and notify you to resolve the conflicts manually. You can see the files with conflicts by running:

```
git status
```

Resolve the conflicts in the affected files, then stage the changes using:

```
git add <file_name>
```

Continue the rebase process with:

```
git rebase --continue
```

The rebase will proceed through the remaining commits. If there are no further conflicts, the rebase will complete successfully. At this point, it is important to force-push the updated branch to the remote repository because history has been rewritten. Use the following command:

```
git push --force
```

For teams working together, communication and coordination about the force-push are crucial to avoid disrupting other developers' workflows.

Squashing commits can streamline the history, making it more approachable and maintaining the repository's cleanliness. This technique is fundamental for software development best practices, ensuring that significant changes are clearly documented and easily traceable.

7.6 Splitting Commits

In certain scenarios, you may find yourself needing to split a single commit into multiple, logically distinct commits. This is particularly useful when the initial commit encompasses multiple unrelated changes, either due to oversight or because it was initially more convenient. Splitting commits enhances the granularity and comprehensibility of the commit history, making it easier for future collaborators to understand the evolution of the codebase.

To begin the process of splitting a commit, we must utilize the interactive rebase command. Assume that we have the following commit history:

```
* c3 - Fix critical bug and add improvement
* c2 - Update documentation
* c1 - Initial commit
```

Here, commit c3 encapsulates two unrelated changes: fixing a critical bug and adding an improvement. To split c3 into two separate commits, follow these steps:

1. Start an interactive rebase, specifying the parent of the commit to split:

```
git rebase -i HEAD~2
```

2. This command opens the default text editor with a list of commits up to HEAD 2. The file will look similar to this:

```
pick c2 Update documentation
pick c3 Fix critical bug and add improvement
```

3. Change the word pick preceding commit c3 to edit. This instructs Git to stop and allow you to amend the commit:

```
pick c2 Update documentation
edit c3 Fix critical bug and add improvement
```

4. Save and close the editor. Git will commence the rebase process and pause at commit c3:

```
Stopped at c3... Fix critical bug and add improvement
You can amend the commit now, with

    git commit --amend

Once you are satisfied with your changes, run

    git rebase --continue
```

5. Proceed by unstaging all the changes from commit c3:

```
git reset HEAD^
```

6. This command reverts the index to the state before commit c3. The working directory remains unchanged, containing all the modifications introduced by c3. Next, selectively add and commit the changes intended for the first split commit, for example, the critical bug fix:

```
git add path/to/bugfix/file1 path/to/bugfix/file2
git commit -m "Fix critical bug"
```

7. Now, stage the remaining changes intended for the second part of the split, for the improvement:

```
git add path/to/improvement/file3 path/to/improvement/file4
git commit -m "Add improvement"
```

8. With the split commits successfully created, continue the rebase process:

```
git rebase --continue
```

9. Git will now replay the remaining commits on top of the newly created ones. The updated commit history will reflect the split commits:

```
* c5 - Add improvement
* c4 - Fix critical bug
* c2 - Update documentation
* c1 - Initial commit
```

During this procedure, be mindful of potential conflicts that might arise when rewriting history. Since splitting a commit effectively alters the commit history, inform collaborators to rebase their work on top of the rewritten branch to prevent discrepancies. Utilizing tools such as gitk or git log to visually inspect the commit history before and after the process can also be helpful in confirming the success of the split operations.

This methodology enables developers to maintain a clean and organized commit history, emphasizing discrete and logical units of work. Such practices are essential for collaborative environments, where clarity and precise documentation of changes significantly streamline code reviews and future maintenance.

7.7 Reflog and Recovering Lost Commits

In Git, the Reflog is an indispensable tool for managing and recovering commits that may appear lost due to various Git operations. The Reflog, short for "reference logs," essentially tracks updates to the tips of branches and other references, providing a history of changes that have occurred. This history includes changes even if they are not part of the current branch's commit history. Understanding how to utilize the Reflog effectively can greatly enhance a developer's ability to recover from seemingly catastrophic errors.

How Reflog Works

Git Reflog records changes to the refs in a repository. This includes events such as commits, rebases, resets, merges, and even branching operations. The logs are stored locally and provide a record of where the references were previously.

To view the Reflog, use the following command:

```
git reflog
```

The output will display a series of entries with the format:

<reflog-index>: <commit-hash> <commit-message>

Each entry represents a state change in the repository, including the commit hash and an associated message describing the change.

Recovering Lost Commits

Consider a scenario where you have performed a reset or an unintended rebase, resulting in the loss of some commits from the visible commit history. Those commits are not permanently deleted; instead, they are still available in the Reflog.

To recover a lost commit, first identify the commit hash from the Reflog output. For instance, you might see an entry like this:

6a2cb5a HEAD@{1}: reset: moving to HEAD^

In this example, the commit hash 6a2cb5a represents the state of the branch before the reset. To recover this commit, perform a hard reset:

```
git reset --hard 6a2cb5a
```

This command will move the head of the branch to the specified commit, effectively restoring the state of the repository to that point.

Using Reflog for Branch Recovery

In some cases, you might inadvertently delete a branch. Considering the Reflog also records branch updates, you can recover a deleted branch using the Reflog.

Assume you deleted a branch named feature-branch. To recover it, find the commit hash from the Reflog that corresponds to the deleted branch:

```
git reflog show feature-branch
```

The output will show entries associated with that branch. Identify the commit hash prior to deletion and use the following command to recreate the branch:

```
git branch feature-branch <commit-hash>
```

By pointing to the appropriate commit hash, you restore the branch to its former state.

Cleaning Up the Reflog

While the Reflog is highly useful for recovering commits, it can grow over time and consume space. Git provides options to prune old entries from the Reflog. To expire entries older than 90 days, use:

```
git reflog expire --expire=90.days
```

To perform more aggressive cleanup, for example expiring entries older than 30 days and performing a garbage collection, the command would be:

```
git reflog expire --expire=30.days --all
git gc --prune=30.days
```

These commands help in maintaining the Reflog's size and ensuring the repository remains efficient.

The Reflog is stored in the .git/logs directory and can be inspected manually if needed. Keep in mind, however, that direct manipulation of Reflog files is not recommended as it can lead to inconsistencies and potential data loss in the repository.

Understanding and leveraging the power of the Reflog significantly enhances one's Git workflow, allowing for effective recovery from errors and refining the management of commit history. Whether dealing with accidental resets, rebases, or deleted branches, the Reflog provides a robust mechanism to revert and recover the intended state of a repository without losing valuable commit information.

7.8 Using Git Bisect for Debugging

The git bisect command is an efficient tool for pinpointing the exact commit that introduced a bug in a Git repository. By performing a binary search through the repository's history, git bisect systematically narrows down the range of commits to identify the one responsible for the issue. This is particularly useful in large repositories where manually checking each commit would be impractical.

To use git bisect, one must first identify a range of commits where the bug was introduced. This requires knowing a good commit (a state when the codebase was functioning correctly) and a bad commit (a state when the bug is present). The command will then perform a binary search within this range. Below, we provide a step-by-step guide to using git bisect.

1. **Starting a bisect session:** Begin the bisect session by running the command:

   ```
   git bisect start
   ```

   This initializes the bisect process and prepares Git for the binary search.

2. **Marking the bad commit:** Identify and mark the commit where the bug was first observed:

   ```
   git bisect bad <bad-commit>
   ```

   Replace <bad-commit> with the actual commit hash of the known bad commit.

3. **Marking the good commit:** Identify and mark the last known good commit where the bug was not present:

   ```
   git bisect good <good-commit>
   ```

   Replace <good-commit> with the commit hash of the known good commit.

   At this point, Git will automatically check out a commit roughly halfway between the good and bad commits, allowing you to test whether the bug is present in that commit.

4. **Testing the chosen commit:** After Git checks out a commit, manually test the code to determine if the bug is present. Based on the results of the test, mark the commit as good or bad:

```
git bisect good
```

if the commit does not exhibit the bug, or:

```
git bisect bad
```

if the bug is present.

5. **Iterating through commits:** Git will continue to check out commits, systematically narrowing down the search space. Repeat the testing and marking process until Git identifies the first bad commit. The following illustrates a typical sequence of commands during a bisect session:

```
Bisecting: 3 revisions left to test after this (roughly 2 steps)
[commit-sha] Commit message
...
git bisect good
Bisecting: 1 revision left to test after this (roughly 1 step)
[commit-sha] Commit message
...
git bisect bad
```

6. **Concluding the bisect session:** Once the offending commit is identified, Git will display the commit hash and accompanying message of the first bad commit. End the bisect session with:

```
git bisect reset
```

This command will return the repository to its original state before the bisect session began.

7. **Automating tests (optional):** For repositories where manual testing is too cumbersome, the process can be automated using a script. Suppose you have a script named test.sh that exits with code 0 for good commits and a non-zero code for bad commits. You can automate the bisect process as follows:

```
git bisect start
git bisect bad <bad-commit>
git bisect good <good-commit>
git bisect run ./test.sh
```

git bisect run will execute the test.sh script for each commit and use its exit status to mark commits as good or bad automatically.

Through the use of git bisect, developers can efficiently identify problematic commits within a large codebase, simplifying the debugging process and saving significant time and effort. The ability to automate the testing process further enhances productivity, especially in large and complex repositories.

7.9 Submodules and Subtrees

Submodules and subtrees provide mechanisms for incorporating external repositories into a project. They support modularization by allowing the integration of separate codebases into a primary repository, facilitating code reuse and collaborative development. Understanding these mechanisms is crucial for managing dependencies efficiently and maintaining a clean project structure.

Submodules

Submodules link to external repositories at specific commits, maintaining a snapshot of the external project within the parent repository. This linkage ensures that the primary project remains consistent with the desired state of its dependencies. To add a submodule, use the following command:

```
git submodule add <repository_url> <path>
```

Here, <repository_url> is the URL of the external repository, and <path> is the directory path where the submodule should reside.

For example, to add a submodule located at https://github.com/example/repo.git into a directory named libs/repo, execute:

```
git submodule add https://github.com/example/repo.git libs/repo
```

This creates an entry in the .gitmodules file, specifying the submodule repository URL and the path within the parent repository. The .gitmodules file might contain:

```
[submodule "libs/repo"]
    path = libs/repo
    url = https://github.com/example/repo.git
```

To initialize and fetch the submodule content, run:

```
git submodule update --init
```

This command ensures that the submodule's working directory is populated with the appropriate files corresponding to its specified commit.

When cloning a repository containing submodules, it's necessary to initialize and update them. Cloning with submodules can be achieved through:

```
git clone --recurse-submodules <repository_url>
```

Or, after cloning:

```
git submodule update --init --recursive
```

These commands bring all submodule contents to the desired state. Submodules require careful management of commits. When updating a submodule, navigate into the submodule directory and perform the necessary commits. After committing changes within the submodule, return to the parent repository and commit the updated submodule reference.

To deinitialize and remove a submodule, this series of commands is employed:

```
git submodule deinit <path_to_submodule>
git rm <path_to_submodule>
rm -rf .git/modules/<path_to_submodule>
```

Subtrees

Subtrees offer an alternative to submodules by maintaining an external repository's code within the parent repository's structure without the complexity of separate submodule management. A subtree embeds the complete history of the external repository as a sub-directory within the main repository.

To add a subtree, use the following command:

```
git subtree add --prefix <directory> <repository_url> <branch>
```

Here, <directory> specifies where the external repository will be added, and <repository_url> is the URL of the external repository. For example, to add the repository https://github.com/example/repo.git into a directory named libs/repo from its main branch:

```
git subtree add --prefix=libs/repo https://github.com/example/repo.git main
```

Unlike submodules, subtrees do not require additional files for defining their inclusion. The external repository's code resides in the specified directory, becoming part of the main repository's history. This integration provides a straightforward way to include external code while maintaining a coherent commit history.

Updating a subtree is accomplished via:

```
git subtree pull --prefix <directory> <repository_url> <branch>
```

This command fetches and merges recent changes from the specified branch of the external repository into the subtree's designated directory. Conversely, to push changes back to the external repository, use:

```
git subtree push --prefix <directory> <repository_url> <branch>
```

Submodules and subtrees each present advantages and trade-offs. Submodules are suitable when the dependency is rarely modified or managed by an independent team. They allow precise control over the dependency's state but introduce complexity in submodule management. Subtrees, while simpler to manage and integrate seamlessly with the main repository's history, result in a larger repository size due to the incorporation of the entire history of dependencies.

Both methods extend Git's capabilities, enabling modular, maintainable project structures that can scale to accommodate complex, collaborative development needs.

7.10 Partial Clones and Shallow Clones

In large-scale projects, managing and maintaining a full clone of a repository can become resource-intensive and unwieldy. Git provides mechanisms such as partial clones and shallow clones to mitigate these issues. These advanced techniques allow users to minimize both disk space usage and network traffic, facilitating more efficient repository interaction.

Partial clones enable working with repositories without having to check out the entire history or all files. This is especially useful for repositories with extensive commit histories or large files that may not be necessary for a user's current tasks. Shallow clones, on the other hand, limit the history depth, reducing storage requirements and speeding up cloning operations.

- **Partial Clones:**

Partial clones utilize the concept of "sparse-checkout" and "partial fetching" to operate more efficiently. Instead of fetching all the objects from the remote repository, partial clones fetch only the objects related to the files of interest. This is achieved through the '–filter' option added to the 'git clone' command. For instance:

```
git clone --filter=blob:none <repository-url>
```

In this example, the '–filter=blob:none' option refrains from downloading any blobs (file content) initially, which is particularly useful for large files that are not immediately needed. Users can later fetch the required objects on-demand using sparse-checkout patterns.

To start working with a subset of the repository, you can configure sparse-checkout:

```
cd <repository-directory>
git sparse-checkout init --cone
git sparse-checkout set <directory-pattern>
```

The '–cone' option simplifies the sparse patterns, and 'set <directory-pattern>' specifies the directories of interest. This enhances performance, especially in CI/CD pipelines or when working with monorepos.

- **Shallow Clones:**

Shallow clones are advantageous when the complete history of a repository is not necessary. By limiting the history depth, Git reduces the amount of data transferred and stored. A shallow clone is created using the '–depth' option with the 'git clone' command as shown below:

```
git clone --depth=1 <repository-url>
```

The '–depth=1' option specifies that only the latest commit is fetched. This significantly trims the clone size and time, which is beneficial for quickly obtaining the most recent snapshot of the repository.

Consider a scenario where you need a little more history, say the last 10 commits:

```
git clone --depth=10 <repository-url>
```

After performing a shallow clone, you may still fetch additional history if needed. For instance, to extend the history depth, use:

```
git fetch --depth=20
```

This command fetches additional commits, extending the history depth to 20. If full history access becomes necessary, the '–unshallow' option transitions the repository to a full clone:

```
git fetch --unshallow
```

- **Combining Partial and Shallow Clones:**

For maximum efficiency, partial and shallow cloning can be combined. Here's an example that demonstrates this combined approach:

```
git clone --depth=1 --filter=blob:none <repository-url>
git sparse-checkout init --cone
git sparse-checkout set <directory-pattern>
```

This strategy minimizes both the history depth and the file set initially checked out. It allows for efficient workload management, especially in environments where network bandwidth and storage resources are constrained.

These advanced cloning techniques align with modern software development practices by facilitating rapid access to necessary components without the overhead of managing the entire repository history or all files. Strategic use of partial and shallow clones can lead to substantial improvements in productivity and resource utilization in complex, large-scale projects. Understanding and implementing these methods should be part of any proficient Git user's toolkit.

Chapter 8

Git Hooks and Automation

This chapter details the use of Git hooks and automation to enhance the development process. It introduces client-side and server-side hooks, explaining how to create and manage them for various use cases. The chapter discusses common hooks such as pre-commit, post-commit, pre-push, and post-push, and demonstrates how to automate workflows effectively. It also addresses security implications and the integration of hooks with other tools to streamline development tasks.

8.1 Introduction to Git Hooks

Git hooks are scripts that Git executes before or after events, such as committing, merging, and receiving updates from a remote repository. These hooks are useful for automating tasks, enforcing policies, and integrating with other tools. By configuring hooks, developers can streamline workflows, ensure code quality, and maintain consistency across different environments.

Git hooks are divided into two main categories: client-side hooks and server-side hooks. Client-side hooks are executed on the user's local environment and trigger on operations such as committing and merging. Server-side hooks run on the remote repository server and are triggered by network operations such as receiving pushed commits. Each hook is managed by placing executable scripts in the hooks directory of the Git repository, typically located at .git/hooks/.

Git hooks can be written in various scripting languages, including Bash, Python, Ruby, and any other language supported by the local environment. By default, Git provides sample hook scripts, but these are deactivated by the .sample extension. To activate a hook, this extension must be removed, and the script must be made executable.

The lifecycle of a Git commit operation involves several potential hook triggers. For instance, before a commit is made, the pre-commit hook can execute scripts to check code formatting or run tests. If the checks succeed, the commit proceeds, and the post-commit hook can then trigger subsequent actions like notifying team members or updating project management systems.

The sequence for a typical commit operation includes the following hooks:

- pre-commit: Executed before the commit is created. Typically used to check for code quality issues.
- prepare-commit-msg: Manipulates the commit message before the commit editor is fired up.
- commit-msg: Validates or modifies the commit message after the commit message has been entered.
- post-commit: Runs after the commit has been created. Often used for notifications or logging.

An example script for the pre-commit hook in Bash might look like this:

```
#!/bin/bash

# Run code linter
eslint .

if [ $? -ne 0 ]; then
  echo "Linting failed. Please fix the issues before committing."
  exit 1
fi

# Run unit tests
npm test

if [ $? -ne 0 ]; then
  echo "Unit tests failed. Please fix the issues before committing."
  exit 1
fi
```

This script runs a code linter and a set of unit tests before allowing the commit. If any of these checks fail, the commit is aborted, and an error message is displayed.

In a large team environment, server-side hooks, such as pre-receive and post-receive, play a crucial role. For instance, the pre-receive hook can enforce policies like ensuring that commit messages follow a specific format, or that all code being pushed has passed the required tests. An example of a pre-receive hook might be:

```
#!/bin/bash

while read oldrev newrev refname; do
  # Check commit messages for compliance
  if ! git log ${oldrev}..${newrev} --pretty=format:%s | grep -qE '^(feat|fix|docs|style|
        refactor|perf|test|chore): '; then
    echo "Error: Your commit messages must follow the conventional commits format."
    exit 1
  fi

  # Run server-side tests
  ./run-server-tests.sh

  if [ $? -ne 0 ]; then
    echo "Error: Tests failed."
    exit 1
  fi
done
```

In this example, each new push is verified to ensure that commit messages follow a specific format, and server-side tests are executed. If any of these checks fail, the push is denied, enforcing policy and maintaining codebase integrity.

Incorporating Git hooks into a development workflow requires configuring each repository's hooks directory and ensuring that every team member has the necessary scripts. Hooks provide a powerful mechanism to automate repetitive tasks, enforce code standards, and integrate with external systems, thereby significantly enhancing the development process. Understanding and utilizing Git hooks effectively can lead to more efficient, error-free, and consistent software development practices.

8.2 Client-Side Hooks

Client-side hooks are scripts that execute on operations originating from the local clone of a Git repository. These hooks are essential for enforcing policies and automating workflows directly on the developer's environment. Each hook corresponds to a particular action, such as preparing a commit message, committing to a repository, or creating an annotated tag. Proper utilization of these hooks can dramatically enhance code quality and streamline local development processes.

- **Pre-commit hook:** The pre-commit hook is invoked before the commit process begins. It is typically used to check the snapshot that is about to be committed, to ensure it adheres to predefined standards. This hook can be an effective tool for catching issues early, such as syntax errors, test failures, or style guide violations.

```
#!/bin/sh

if grep -q 'debugger' staging/*; then
  echo "Commit contains debugger statements."
  exit 1
fi
```

Upon detecting a debugger statement in the staged files, this script aborts the commit process and prints an error message. Integrating such checks helps foster cleaner, more maintainable code.

- **Prepare-commit-msg hook:** The prepare-commit-msg hook is executed after the default commit message is created, but before the commit message editor is fired up. Its common usages include adding a branch name to the commit message or appending template text to the commit message.

```
#!/bin/sh

BRANCH_NAME=$(git symbolic-ref --short HEAD)
FILE=$1

if ! grep -q "\[$BRANCH_NAME\]" $FILE; then
  sed -i.bak -e "1s/^/[$BRANCH_NAME] /" $FILE
fi
```

This script appends the current branch name to the beginning of the commit message, ensuring that commit messages within specific branches are traceable and context-aware.

- **Commit-msg hook:** Once the commit message is prepared, the commit-msg hook runs. It's primarily used for committing message validation, such as enforcing message format rules like the length of lines, presence of a ticket number, etc.

```
#!/bin/sh

MSG_FILE=$1
FORBIDDEN_PHRASE="WIP"

if grep -iq "$FORBIDDEN_PHRASE" "$MSG_FILE"; then
  echo "Commit message contains forbidden phrase: $FORBIDDEN_PHRASE"
  exit 1
fi
```

This hook ensures that commit messages do not contain the phrase "WIP", thus preventing work-in-progress commits that may have unintended side effects.

- **Post-commit hook:** The post-commit hook is useful for notifying external systems (e.g., CI servers) about new commits, updating logs, or performing any action that must occur after a commit has been recorded in the local repository.

```
#!/bin/sh

COMMIT_HASH=$(git rev-parse --short HEAD)
curl -X POST -H "Content-Type: application/json" \
     -d "{\"commit\": \"$COMMIT_HASH\"}" \
     https://example.com/notify
```

By sending a notification to an external server, this script ensures that other systems can react to new commits in real-time. It is crucial for keeping downstream services updated with the latest changes.

- **Pre-push hook:** During a push operation, the pre-push hook is invoked to facilitate pre-push safety checks, such as running tests or verifying that the local repository is in a consistent state before changes are sent to the remote repository.

```
#!/bin/sh

REMOTE="$1"
URL="$2"

if ! make test; then
  echo "Tests failed."
  exit 1
fi
```

Executing the project's test suite prior to pushing ensures that the developer does not accidentally push changes that break functionality. This promotes a higher level of code integrity and reliability.

Properly configured client-side hooks can significantly improve the development experience, enforcing local compliance with standards, catching errors early, and providing immediate feedback. These preliminary checks can prevent problematic code from propagating to shared repositories, ensuring a stable and healthy codebase.

8.3 Server-Side Hooks

Server-side hooks are custom scripts that run on the server where a Git repository is hosted. They are triggered by specific actions during the repository's lifecycle, such as receiving a push from a client. Server-side hooks are essential for enforcing policies, automating tasks, and enhancing the overall workflow of development teams. This section delves into the various server-side hooks available, their purposes, and how to implement them effectively.

The primary server-side hooks include pre-receive, update, and post-receive. These hooks enable administrators to control the integrity of the repository by preventing corrupt or non-compliant commits, notifying teams of changes, and triggering CI/CD pipelines.

The pre-receive hook is executed before any refs are updated in the repository. This hook can be used to enforce commit policies, check for proper commit messages, or validate other repository-specific rules. If any checks fail, the push is rejected and the changes are not applied.

```
#!/bin/bash
# pre-receive hook example

# Read ref updates from stdin
while read oldrev newrev refname
do
    # Check if the ref being updated is the master branch
    if [[ "$refname" == "refs/heads/master" ]]; then
        # Enforce commit message policy
        if ! git rev-list $newrev | grep -qE '^[a-z]{5,30}'; then
            echo "Aborting push: commit messages must be between 5 and 30 characters
                long."
            exit 1
        fi
    fi
done

exit 0
```

The update hook is triggered once for each branch that is being pushed to, rather than once for the entire push operation. This finer granularity allows for more focused checks and actions on individual branches.

```
#!/bin/bash
# update hook example

refname=$1
oldrev=$2
newrev=$3

# Allow force-pushes to non-protected branches but deny them for protected branches
if [[ "$refname" =~ ^refs/heads/(master|main|develop)$ ]]; then
    if ! git merge-base --is-ancestor $oldrev $newrev; then
        echo "Force push to protected branch $refname is denied!"
        exit 1
    fi
fi

exit 0
```

The post-receive hook runs after the entire push operation has completed, making it appropriate for tasks that should occur once the push has been successfully applied. Common usages include notifying team members of changes, triggering CI/CD pipelines, or updating issue trackers.

```
#!/bin/bash
# post-receive hook example

# Read ref updates from stdin
while read oldrev newrev refname
do
    # Notify team members of changes to the master branch
    if [[ "$refname" == "refs/heads/master" ]]; then
        curl -X POST -H 'Content-type: application/json' \
        --data '{"text":"The master branch has been updated."}' \
        https://hooks.slack.com/services/your/webhook/url
    fi
done

exit 0
```

These script examples illustrate how server-side hooks can be customized to enforce policies and automate repetitive tasks. They are an integral part of a robust Git repository management strategy.

Implementing server-side hooks requires administrative access to the repository server. Hooks should be placed in the hooks directory of the bare repository, and they must be executable. For instance:

```
chmod +x hooks/pre-receive
```

Careful attention must be paid to the performance and reliability of hook scripts, as they can impact the speed and success of push operations. Hooks should be efficient and error-handled to avoid unintended disruptions to the workflow. Regularly reviewing and updating hooks ensures they remain aligned with project policies and technological advancements.

Server-side hook scripts are a powerful feature, providing administrators with the necessary tools to maintain the integrity and efficiency of the Git repository. Properly leveraged, they can significantly enhance the development process by automating checks and actions that would otherwise require manual intervention.

8.4 Creating and Managing Hooks

Git hooks are scripts that Git automatically executes before or after certain events such as commit, push, and receive. To create and manage these hooks effectively, it is essential to understand their structure, default locations, and execution contexts. This section will delve into the specifics of creating hooks, managing them in a repository, and some best practices for maintaining hooks in larger teams or projects.

By default, Git stores its hooks in the .git/hooks directory of your repository. Each hook is a simple script that can be written in any scripting language, such as Bash, Python, or Perl, as long as the script is executable. Git provides sample hook scripts in this directory with a .sample extension.

To create a new hook, perform the following steps:

1. **Navigate to the .git/hooks directory:**

   ```
   cd path/to/your/repo/.git/hooks
   ```

2. **Choose a hook type and create a script:** Decide which hook you want to implement. For example, a pre-commit hook script can be created with the following command:

   `touch pre-commit`Ensure the script has no file extension to be recognized by Git as a hook.

3. **Write the script:** Open the script in your favorite text editor and add your scripting logic. For instance, a simple Bash script to check for TODO comments before allowing a commit might look like this:

```
#!/bin/bash

if grep -rn "TODO" .; then
    echo "Error: Please resolve all TODO comments before committing."
```

```
    exit 1
fi
```

4. **Make the script executable:** Once you've written your hook script, you need to make it executable:

   ```
   chmod +x pre-commit
   ```

The script is now ready to be executed by Git under the appropriate conditions. However, it's good practice to manage and version your hooks effectively, especially in collaborative environments.

Managing Hooks Across a Repository

To ensure consistency across development environments, hooks should be shared among all contributors. One way to manage hooks is to store them in a version-controlled directory separate from .git/hooks. For example, you could create a hooks directory at the root of your repository and include this in your version control:

```
mkdir hooks
```

Move all your custom hook scripts to this directory:

```
mv .git/hooks/pre-commit hooks/pre-commit
```

Now, users need to create symbolic links in .git/hooks pointing to these version-controlled scripts:

```
ln -s ../../hooks/pre-commit .git/hooks/pre-commit
```

To automate the linking process and ensure all developers set up the hooks correctly, you can provide a setup script in the repository. For example, a setup script in setup-hooks.sh might look like this:

```
#!/bin/bash

HOOK_NAMES=("pre-commit" "post-commit" "pre-push" "post-push")

for hook in "${HOOK_NAMES[@]}"; do
    if [ -f "hooks/$hook" ]; then
        ln -sf ../../hooks/$hook .git/hooks/$hook
        echo "Linked $hook hook"
    fi
done
```

Make this script executable:

```
chmod +x setup-hooks.sh
```

Instruct all repository contributors to execute this script after cloning the repository to ensure hooks are properly linked:

```
./setup-hooks.sh
```

Maintaining and Updating Hooks

Keeping hook scripts up to date and ensuring all contributors have the latest versions is crucial. Encourage a workflow where updates to hook scripts are merged through pull requests, and communicate the importance of running the setup script after pulling new changes.

To further automate this process, consider integrating hook setups into your continuous integration (CI) pipeline to catch any discrepancies early. For example, using a tool like Jenkins or GitHub Actions can help ensure that the hooks are functioning correctly across all environments without requiring manual intervention.

Documenting the purpose and behavior of each hook script in a README file within the hooks directory can also be helpful for new contributors. This documentation should include the expected environment and dependencies for running each script, as well as any specific instructions for setup and use.

By following these practices, you can create a robust and maintainable system for managing Git hooks, ensuring consistency and efficiency across your development team.

8.5 Common Use Cases for Hooks

Git hooks provide a powerful mechanism to automate tasks and enforce policies during various stages of the Git workflow. Here, we will explore some typical use cases for hooks that can enhance development processes, ensure code quality, and streamline team collaboration.

One prevalent use case for Git hooks is enforcing coding standards before code is committed to the repository. The pre-commit hook is ideal for this purpose. By integrating linters and formatters, such as ESLint for JavaScript or Black for Python, into the pre-commit hook, developers can automatically check for syntax errors, enforce style guidelines, and reformat code before it gets committed. This helps maintain a consistent codebase, reduces stylistic discrepancies, and catches potential issues early in the development cycle.

```
#!/bin/sh
# Pre-commit hook to check Python code formatting using Black
black --check .
if [ $? -ne 0 ]; then
  echo "Error: Python files are not formatted correctly. Please run 'black .' and try
```

```
    again."
  exit 1
fi
```

Another common use case is running tests automatically before changes are pushed to the remote repository. This can be accomplished using the pre-push hook. By integrating unit tests, integration tests, or end-to-end tests into the pre-push hook, teams can ensure that only code that passes all tests gets merged into the remote repository. This mitigates the risk of introducing bugs or breaking functionality in shared branches.

```
#!/bin/sh
# Pre-push hook to run tests
npm test
if [ $? -ne 0 ]; then
  echo "Error: Tests failed. Please fix the issues and try again."
  exit 1
fi
```

Developers often use Git hooks to enforce security policies. The pre-commit or pre-push hooks can be employed to scan for sensitive information like passwords or API keys before they are committed or pushed to a repository. Tools like git-secrets can be integrated within these hooks to automatically detect and prevent sensitive data from being inadvertently shared.

```
#!/bin/sh
# Pre-commit hook to check for sensitive information using git-secrets
git secrets --scan
if [ $? -ne 0 ]; then
  echo "Error: Sensitive information detected. Please remove it and try again."
  exit 1
fi
```

Hooks can also facilitate communication and collaboration within a team. The post-commit hook can be utilized to notify team members of new commits via email or a messaging platform like Slack. This is particularly useful in continuous integration/continuous deployment (CI/CD) environments, where it is crucial to keep team members informed of ongoing changes.

```
#!/bin/sh
# Post-commit hook to send a Slack notification
commit_message=$(git log -1 --pretty=%B)
author=$(git log -1 --pretty=format:'%an')
curl -X POST -H 'Content-type: application/json' --data "{
  \"text\": \"New commit by $author: $commit_message\"
}" https://hooks.slack.com/services/T00000000/B00000000/
     XXXXXXXXXXXXXXXXXXXXXXXX
```

Moreover, hooks can be instrumental in managing repository metadata. The post-receive hook, a server-side hook, is commonly used to update an application deployment or trigger CI/CD pipelines after changes are pushed to a central repository. For example, it can pull changes to a staging server, run deployment scripts, or notify an external CI/CD system to start execution.

```
#!/bin/sh
# Post-receive hook to deploy updates to a staging server
while read oldrev newrev ref
do
  branch=$(echo $ref | sed 's,.*/,,')
  if [ "$branch" == "main" ]; then
    git --work-tree=/path/to/deployment --git-dir=/path/to/repo checkout -f $branch
    /path/to/deployment/scripts/deploy.sh
  fi
done
```

Git hooks can be tailored to specific workflows, making them invaluable tools in a developer's toolkit. By automating routine tasks, enforcing policies, and facilitating better team communication, hooks ensure that software development processes are more efficient, reliable, and collaborative. Through proper implementation and management, Git hooks can significantly enhance the robustness and maintainability of codebases.

8.6 Pre-Commit and Post-Commit Hooks

Pre-commit and post-commit hooks are integral parts of the Git automation process, offering developers robust mechanisms to ensure code quality, enforce policies, and streamline workflows. These hooks allow for operations to be executed at critical points in the commit lifecycle, providing a framework for integrating a variety of tools and processes.

The pre-commit hook is triggered before a commit is finalized. It runs scripts designed to inspect the state of the codebase, allowing for preventative actions to be taken if certain criteria are not met. This can include running linters, static analysis tools, or custom validation scripts which can halt the commit process when issues are detected. To create a pre-commit hook, place an executable script in the .git/hooks/ directory named pre-commit.

Example of a pre-commit script that checks for Python syntax errors:

```
#!/bin/sh

# Check for Python files with syntax errors
```

```
for file in $(git diff --cached --name-only --diff-filter=ACM | grep '\.py$')
do
    python -m py_compile "$file"
    if [ $? -ne 0 ]; then
        echo "Syntax errors detected in $file. Commit aborted."
        exit 1
    fi
done

exit 0
```

This script fetches the list of staged Python files and runs python -m py_compile on each one to detect syntax errors. If a syntax error is found, the commit is aborted, and an error message is displayed.

The benefits of implementing a pre-commit hook are numerous. Common tasks include:

- Linting code to enforce style guidelines (e.g., using eslint for JavaScript).
- Running unit tests to ensure new changes do not break the existing functionality.
- Checking for forbidden or sensitive keywords.
- Automatically formatting code using tools like prettier or black.

The post-commit hook is executed after a commit has been completed. This hook is useful for actions that should occur once the changes are safely recorded in the local repository. Some typical uses include updating issue trackers, sending notifications, or performing local repository maintenance.

To set up a post-commit hook, create an executable script named post-commit in the .git/hooks/ directory.

Example of a post-commit script to send a notification email upon successful commit:

```
#!/bin/sh

# Email variables
RECIPIENT="developer@example.com"
SUBJECT="New Commit Notification"
BODY="A new commit has been made to the repository."

# Create a basic email message
echo "$BODY" | mail -s "$SUBJECT" "$RECIPIENT"

exit 0
```

This script sends an email notification to a specified recipient whenever a new commit is completed. The standard mail command is utilized to dispatch the email.

Key considerations when using post-commit hooks:

- Avoiding long-running tasks that could delay the developer experience.
- Ensuring that scripts are idempotent to prevent issues in the case of repeated executions.
- Adequately handling errors to prevent silent failures.

Together, pre-commit and post-commit hooks form a foundational part of Git-based automation, ensuring quality control right at the developer's workstation while facilitating broader team communication and integration. Hooks provide a straightforward yet powerful mechanism for embedding quality control, security checks, and various maintenance tasks directly into the workflow, thereby enhancing overall efficiency and reliability of the development process.

8.7 Pre-Push and Post-Push Hooks

Pre-push and post-push hooks in Git are critical mechanisms for automating tasks related to the act of pushing changes to a remote repository. These hooks allow developers to enforce policies and perform essential checks or tasks before and after the push operation, thereby maintaining code integrity and streamlined workflows.

The pre-push hook is invoked by git push and is executed before the push action takes place. This hook receives a list of references that are being pushed, giving the user an opportunity to validate or reject the push transaction based on predefined criteria. If the pre-push hook exits with a non-zero status, the push is aborted. This hook is particularly useful for preventing potentially harmful changes from being integrated into the remote repository.

```
#!/bin/sh

# Validate the proposed push to the remote
remote="$1"
url="$2"

while read local_ref local_sha remote_ref remote_sha
```

```
do
    if [ ${local_ref} = "refs/heads/main" ]; then
        echo "Pushing to the main branch is restricted."
        exit 1
    fi
done

exit 0
```

In the example above, the pre-push hook reads the local and remote references and restricts pushes to the main branch. This safety mechanism ensures that a careless push to a critical branch is prevented. The script maintains simplicity and efficiency, only performing checks relevant to the push.

The post-push hook is executed after the push is completed, making it suitable for operations that should be performed subsequent to a successful push, such as notifications or logging. Unlike the pre-push hook, the post-push hook is not built-in to Git by default, but it can be implemented as a custom solution within a Git hosting service or by other means such as continuous integration (CI) systems.

```
#!/bin/sh

# This script should be manually invoked post-push
log_file="/path/to/log_file.txt"

echo "Push to remote repository completed at $(date)" >> ${log_file}
```

In this example, the custom post-push script logs the timestamp of a successful push to a specified file. While simplistic, it demonstrates how additional actions can be automated after a push, such as logging, notifications, or triggering subsequent workflows.

By leveraging pre-push and post-push hooks effectively, teams can enforce stringent checks and ensure critical post-push actions are consistently executed. This use of automation bolsters the robustness of the development workflow, significantly reducing human error and intervention.

8.8 Automating Workflows with Hooks

Automating workflows with hooks in Git provides great potential to streamline development, enforce policies, and ensure consistent practices within a team. By leveraging hooks, repetitive tasks can be automated, reducing the manual overhead and minimizing the risk of human error. Hooks serve as integrated scripts that are triggered by specific actions, making them powerful tools in a developer's toolkit. This section discusses various ways to automate workflows with hooks, focusing on practical examples to illustrate their utility and effectiveness.

Consider a scenario where a team needs to enforce code formatting standards. This can be achieved by automating the process through a pre-commit hook. The pre-commit hook can be configured to run a linter or formatter before a commit is allowed. This ensures all code adheres to a predefined style, reducing the risk of formatting-related issues.

```
#!/bin/sh
# A sample pre-commit hook script to format code using clang-format

# Specify the files to format
FILES=$(git diff --cached --name-only --diff-filter=d | grep -E '\.(c|cpp|h)$')
if [ "$FILES" != "" ]; then
    echo "Formatting C/C++ source files..."
    for file in $FILES
    do
        clang-format -i $file
        git add $file
    done
    echo "Completed formatting."
else
    echo "No C/C++ source files to format."
fi
```

This script first identifies staged files with extensions '.c', '.cpp', or '.h'. For each file, it applies 'clang-format' and stages the formatted file. By automating this task, each commit complies with the project's formatting standards without requiring manual intervention.

Similarly, pre-push hooks can automate checks to ensure code quality before changes are pushed to the remote repository. For instance, running unit tests every time a developer attempts to push can prevent broken code from being integrated.

```
#!/bin/sh
# A sample pre-push hook script to run unit tests

echo "Running unit tests..."
npm test
if [ $? -ne 0 ]; then
    echo "Unit tests failed. Aborting push."
    exit 1
else
    echo "Unit tests passed. Proceeding with push."
    exit 0
fi
```

In this script, the 'npm test' command runs the unit tests. If the tests fail (indicated by a non-zero exit code), the push is aborted. This ensures that only code passing the unit tests reaches the remote repository, maintaining a higher quality codebase.

Server-side hooks, such as the 'post-receive' hook, can automate workflows associated with the deployment process. Automating deployment can help ensure consistency and reliability. A common use case is initiating a deployment process upon receiving new changes in the repository.

```
#!/bin/sh
# Post-receive hook to deploy application on code push

DEPLOY_DIR="/var/www/myapp"
GIT_DIR="/home/git/repositories/myapp.git"

echo "Deploying application..."
cd $DEPLOY_DIR || exit
unset GIT_DIR
git pull origin main || exit
./deploy.sh || exit
echo "Deployment successful."
```

In the 'post-receive' hook script above, the working directory for the application deployment is specified. The script navigates to this directory, pulls the latest changes from the main branch, and initiates the deployment process via a custom deployment script 'deploy.sh'. This automated strategy ensures that deployments occur smoothly and consistently each time new code is pushed.

Integrating hooks with other tools can further enhance automation. Consider combining a pre-commit hook with a continuous integration tool. This integration can automatically trigger a build and run tests on a continuous integration server, such as Jenkins or GitLab CI, providing immediate feedback to developers.

Additionally, hooks can be used to enforce security-related policies. For example, an 'update' hook on the server can prevent sensitive information, like secret keys or passwords, from being pushed to the repository by scanning the commit content.

The following example demonstrates implementing a pre-receive hook to scan for sensitive information using 'git-secrets':

```
#!/bin/sh
# A sample pre-receive hook script to enforce security checks using git-secrets

while read oldrev newrev refname
do
    # Check all commits introduced by the push
    if ! git secrets --scan $oldrev..$newrev; then
        echo "Commit contains sensitive information. Aborting push."
```

```
        exit 1
    fi
done
exit 0
```

By integrating 'git-secrets', this hook scans all commits introduced by a push for sensitive information. If any is found, the push is aborted, preventing accidental leaks of confidential data.

When automating workflows with hooks, it is essential to consider the impact on developer productivity and workflow complexity. While hooks add valuable automated checks and balances, they must be carefully designed to provide value without becoming a hindrance. Proper documentation and communication within the team about the hooks in use and their purpose can enhance acceptance and collaboration.

Each hook should be thoroughly tested before widespread deployment to ensure it performs as expected under various scenarios. This minimizes disruptions to the development workflow and avoids unnecessary delays.

Automating workflows with hooks in Git plays a crucial role in achieving high code quality, enforcing standards, and maintaining security. By embedding these automated processes directly into the development lifecycle, teams can focus more on innovation and less on repetitive tasks, ensuring a smoother and more reliable path from code commit to deployment.

8.9 Security Implications of Using Hooks

The implementation of Git hooks introduces potential security risks that must be rigorously managed to ensure the integrity and security of the development process. Git hooks, by design, execute scripts automatically at various points in the version control workflow. While this automation facilitates efficiency and error reduction, it concurrently creates attack vectors that could be exploited by malicious actors. Several security considerations are paramount when utilizing Git hooks, and these are discussed herein to provide a comprehensive understanding of the risks and the measures necessary to mitigate them.

First and foremost, the execution context of Git hooks is crucial. Hooks typically run with the permissions of the user who invokes the Git command that triggers the hook, which could lead to privilege escalation scenarios. If a hook script executes unintended or malicious code, it can perform operations with the same access level as the user, potentially compromising the system. To mitigate this, it is essential to adhere to the principle of least privilege, ensuring that scripts perform only the necessary operations required for the hook's functionality.

Another significant risk arises from the source and modification of hook scripts. Since hooks are local to an individual repository, there exists the possibility that scripts can be modified or replaced with malicious versions. To prevent unauthorized changes, it is advisable to use version control mechanisms for the hooks themselves, maintaining them in a secure, centralized repository with controlled access permissions. Additionally, employing cryptographic signing can help verify the authenticity and integrity of hook scripts before their execution.

The contents of hook scripts should be scrutinized rigorously. Scripts should be audited for potentially harmful commands and constructs, such as shell commands that can alter the file system or network operations that might exfiltrate data. Static code analysis tools can be used to scan scripts for vulnerabilities and best practice violations. Moreover, adopting a review process for changes to hook scripts ensures that no harmful code is inadvertently introduced.

Isolation of the execution environment is another effective strategy to limit the potential impact of a compromised hook. Running hooks in a containerized or sandboxed environment can provide a controlled and confined execution context, reducing the risk that a hook script could affect the broader system. This approach is particularly beneficial in scenarios where hooks need to perform complex or potentially risky operations.

The security of external dependencies used within hooks also warrants attention. Many hook scripts rely on external libraries and tools, which can introduce vulnerabilities if not managed properly. Regularly updating dependencies and using reputable sources reduces the chances of introducing security weaknesses. It is also good practice to pin dependencies to specific versions known to be secure, preventing unexpected behavior due to unverified updates.

From an organizational perspective, defining clear policies around the use of hooks can help enforce security best practices. Policies should include guidelines on creating, reviewing, and maintaining hook scripts, as well as specifying acceptable uses of hooks. Training and awareness programs can educate developers on the security implications of hooks and promote a culture of security-conscious development practices.

Consideration must also be given to server-side hooks, which operate on the remote repository and can affect multiple users. Server-side hooks, such as pre-receive or update, should be monitored closely and restricted to trusted administrators. Implementing logging and alerting mechanisms around the execution of server-side hooks can provide visibility into their usage and help detect any anomalous or unauthorized activities.

The deployment pipeline should incorporate safeguards to validate and enforce the correct behavior of hooks. Automated tests can check the functionality of hooks in an isolated environment before they are deployed to production repositories. Continuous integration and continuous deployment (CI/CD) workflows should include steps to validate the integrity and performance of all hook scripts involved.

Understanding the broader ecosystem in which Git operates is also key to managing the security of hooks. Integrations with other tools, such as code linters, CI/CD systems, and dependency managers, introduce additional vectors that can impact the security posture. Ensuring that these tools are securely configured and that interactions between them and the Git hooks are properly authenticated and authorized is critical. For instance, when a hook script interfaces with a CI/CD system, using secure tokens or keys for authentication prevents unauthorized access.

To encapsulate the discussions on security, practical implementation of secure Git hooks should focus on permissions, source control, script content scrutiny, execution environment isolation, dependency management, organizational policies, strict monitoring of server-side hooks, robust deployment testing, and secure integration with the broader ecosystem. Each facet requires vigilant attention to detail and adherence to security best practices to effectively mitigate the inherent risks of using Git hooks.

8.10 Integrating Hooks with Other Tools

Integrating Git hooks with other tools can significantly enhance the development process by automating tasks, ensuring code quality, and facilitating continuous integration and delivery (CI/CD). This section delves into practical approaches for integrating Git hooks with various tools, covering linting, testing frameworks, CI/CD pipelines, and deployment tools, among others.

To begin with, consider the implementation of linting in the commit process. Linting helps identify potential errors and enforce coding styles. The integration of a linter with the pre-commit hook ensures that only code adhering to the specified standards is committed. For example, using a Python linter, the pre-commit script might look like this:

```
#!/bin/bash
# Pre-commit hook to run pylint
FILES=$(git diff --cached --name-only --diff-filter=ACM | grep '\.py$')
if [ -n "$FILES" ]; then
    pylint $FILES
    if [ $? -ne 0 ]; then
        echo "Pylint check failed. Commit aborted."
        exit 1
    fi
fi
exit 0
```

The script retrieves the modified Python files in the staging area and runs pylint on each file. If pylint finds issues, the commit is aborted, adhering to the policy of committing only high-quality code.

Testing is another crucial aspect of software development that can be streamlined with hooks. A pre-push hook can be employed to run test suites before code is pushed to a remote repository. This ensures that the codebase remains stable and free from critical bugs. An example pre-push script to run tests using a testing framework like pytest could be:

```
#!/bin/bash
# Pre-push hook to run pytest
pytest
if [ $? -ne 0 ]; then
    echo "Tests failed. Push aborted."
    exit 1
fi
exit 0
```

By integrating this script, developers can automatically verify that their changes pass all tests before updating the remote repository, maintaining the integrity of the shared codebase.

Beyond linting and testing, Git hooks can be integrated with CI/CD tools such as Jenkins, GitLab CI, or GitHub Actions. These integrations can trigger automated builds and deployments, enhancing the development workflow. A common scenario involves configuring a post-commit or post-push hook to notify a CI/CD server to start a build process. A simplified example using a post-push hook to trigger Jenkins might look like this:

```
#!/bin/bash
# Post-push hook to trigger Jenkins build
JENKINS_URL="http://jenkins-server/job/myproject/build?token=MY_TOKEN"
```

```
curl -X POST $JENKINS_URL
```

This script sends a POST request to the Jenkins server's build endpoint, initiating a build whenever changes are pushed to the repository.

For deployment, hooks can be invaluable in automating the release process. For instance, the post-receive hook on the server-side can be used to deploy code to a production server. An example of a post-receive script for an automated deployment might look like this:

```
#!/bin/bash
# Post-receive hook for automated deployment
DEPLOY_DIR="/var/www/myproject"
GIT_DIR="${DEPLOY_DIR}/.git"
BRANCH="main"
TARGET_DIR="${DEPLOY_DIR}/current"

while read oldrev newrev ref
do
    if [[ $ref = refs/heads/$BRANCH ]];
    then
        # Deploy the branch to the target directory
        GIT_WORK_TREE=$TARGET_DIR git checkout -f $BRANCH
        echo "Deployed branch $BRANCH to $TARGET_DIR"
    fi
done
```

This script checks out the latest code from the specified branch to the deployment directory, effectively updating the deployment whenever code is pushed to the repository.

Moreover, integrating hooks with code quality tools such as SonarQube can continuously monitor code quality and maintain high standards. For instance, a pre-push hook can be set to run a SonarQube scan:

```
#!/bin/bash
# Pre-push hook to run SonarQube scan
SONAR_SCANNER="/path/to/sonar-scanner"
$SONAR_SCANNER
if [ $? -ne 0 ]; then
    echo "SonarQube scan failed. Push aborted."
    exit 1
fi
exit 0
```

Running a SonarQube scan before pushing ensures that code quality metrics meet the defined thresholds, preventing code with significant issues from being integrated into the main codebase.

By integrating Git hooks with other tools, developers can automate numerous tasks, enhance code quality, and streamline the development pipeline. This not only increases efficiency but also ensures a consistent and reliable codebase, fostering a robust development environment.

Chapter 9

Troubleshooting and Debugging

This chapter provides strategies for troubleshooting and debugging in Git. It covers common Git errors and their solutions, using commands like git status and git log for diagnosing issues, and resolving merge conflicts. The chapter also explains how to recover lost commits with reflog, fix mistakes using git reset and revert, and handle the detached HEAD state. Additionally, it includes techniques for debugging with git bisect, restoring deleted branches, and verifying repository integrity.

9.1 Introduction to Troubleshooting

Troubleshooting in Git involves diagnosing and addressing issues that may arise during version control operations. This section focuses on equipping users with the necessary skills to identify the root causes of common problems and apply appropriate solutions. Git, although a robust version control system, can present complex challenges, particularly in collaborative environments or large projects. Understanding these challenges and their resolution is fundamental for effective version control.

During the routine use of Git, users might encounter various issues such as merge conflicts, lost commits, or a detached HEAD state. Each of these issues, if not resolved promptly, can lead to workflow interruptions and potential data loss. Therefore, a systematic approach to troubleshooting is essential.

A vital first step in troubleshooting is familiarization with key Git commands that aid in diagnosing issues. These include:

- git status: Provides the current status of the working directory and staging area.
- git log: Shows the commit history for the repository.
- git diff: Displays differences between commits and working directory changes.
- git reflog: Tracks updates to the repository's reference logs.
- git bisect: Helps in identifying the specific commit that introduced a bug by binary search.

When a problem arises, the first command to execute is git status. This command outputs the current state of the working directory and the staging area, highlighting any changes that are staged for commit, untracked files, and any pending merges. For example:

```
$ git status
On branch main
Your branch is up to date with 'origin/main'.

Changes to be committed:
  (use "git reset HEAD <file>..." to unstage)
        modified: file1.txt

Untracked files:
  (use "git add <file>..." to include in what will be committed)
        newfile.txt
```

In this output, we observe that file1.txt has been modified and staged for commit, while newfile.txt remains untracked. This command is invaluable for quickly assessing the state of the repository and identifying discrepancies that need attention.

For deeper insights into the history of changes, git log can be used. It displays a list of commits, providing details such as commit hashes, authors, dates, and commit messages. An example usage is shown below:

```
$ git log
commit 1d5f3e3b1e8e8dc0c47e1d6a2bad123456789012
Author: Jane Doe <jane.doe@example.com>
```

```
Date: Fri Oct 1 12:34:56 2023 +0200

    Fix bug in user authentication

commit 0c4e2e1b1e0d8bc0a4d9e9b2a123987654321abc
Author: John Smith <john.smith@example.com>
Date: Thu Sep 30 11:23:45 2023 +0200

    Improve performance of data processing
```

This output lists recent commits, making it easier to track changes and identify potential sources of issues. Advanced options for git log allow filtering and formatting the output, which can aid in pinpointing specific problems.

The git diff command shows differences between commits, working directory changes, and staging area changes. This is crucial for understanding what has been altered and evaluating potential conflicts. For instance:

```
$ git diff HEAD~1 HEAD
diff --git a/file1.txt b/file1.txt
index 83e24ab..e4f4731 100644
--- a/file1.txt
+++ b/file1.txt
@@ -1,4 +1,4 @@
-Original line
+Modified line
 Another line
```

This example highlights changes in file1.txt between the last commit and the current state, showing that "Original line" was replaced with "Modified line". Understanding such differences is critical in resolving conflicts and debugging erroneous commits.

For recovering lost commits and tracking changes, git reflog is instrumental. Reflog maintains a history of the changes to the tips of branches and other references. This command can reveal the commits that might not be visible through git log due to branch moves or resets:

```
$ git reflog
1d5f3e3 HEAD@{0}: commit: Fix bug in user authentication
c4e2e1b HEAD@{1}: checkout: moving from main to feature-branch
```

From this output, we observe the recent activities on the repository, including a commit and a branch switch. This historical data is useful for recovery operations, such as restoring lost commits.

Finally, when faced with bugs, git bisect automates the process of detecting the commit that introduced the fault by conducting a binary search between known good and bad commits. This command systematically checks out and tests commits, significantly speeding up the debugging process. The procedure begins with initiating the bisect:

```
$ git bisect start
$ git bisect bad
$ git bisect good <commit-hash>
```

The commands above mark the current state as bad and a known good commit. Git subsequently checks out intermediary commits for testing until the problematic commit is identified.

Effective troubleshooting always involves a clear, systematic approach using the appropriate Git tools and commands. Understanding these commands and their outputs is essential for diagnosing issues accurately and efficiently in any Git-based project.

9.2 Common Git Errors and Solutions

When working with Git, encountering various errors and issues is inevitable. This section aims to provide comprehensive solutions to some of the most common Git errors. Understanding these errors and their resolutions will enhance your proficiency in effectively using Git.

The first error to address is the *detached HEAD state*. This state can occur when a commit is checked out directly or a previous commit is accessed. The detached HEAD state is diagnostically useful but can create confusion with newer users.

To address a detached HEAD state, the status of the repository must be understood:

```
git status
```

If the HEAD is detached, it can be reattached to a branch:

```
# Assuming reattachment to the main branch
git checkout main
```

Alternatively, to create a new branch from the current commit and reattach:

```
git checkout -b new-branch-name
```

Another common error is the ***merge conflict***. Merge conflicts occur when Git is unable to automatically reconcile differences between branches. During a merge attempt, if conflicts are present, Git will indicate files that need attention:

```
/project/path/file1.txt: needs merge
/project/path/file2.txt: needs merge
```

To resolve these conflicts, the files must be manually edited to determine the final content. This can be done by opening each conflicted file:

```
<<<<<< HEAD
Your changes here
======
Changes from the other branch here
>>>>>> branch-name
```

Once resolved, mark the conflicts as resolved:

```
git add /project/path/file1.txt
git add /project/path/file2.txt
```

Following this, the merge process can be completed:

```
git commit -m "Merge conflict resolved"
```

The ***error: cannot fast-forward*** often occurs during a fetch or pull operation. This happens when there are changes on both the local and remote branches that need to be manually merged. To resolve this:

```
git fetch origin
git merge origin/main
```

For situations where the error is encountered due to non-fast-forward updates, resetting the local branch to match the remote repository can be necessary:

```
git reset --hard origin/main
```

Handling *untracked files* or *file modifications* that are not wanted in the commit can also pose issues. Using git stash can temporarily remove changes from the working directory:

```
git stash
```

To reapply the stashed changes:

```
git stash apply
```

Or to apply and remove them from the stash list:

```
git stash pop
```

In cases of accidental commit, the *git reset* command can revert changes:

```
# To uncommit but keep changes staged
git reset --soft HEAD~1

# To uncommit and unstage changes
git reset --mixed HEAD~1

# To uncommit and discard all changes
git reset --hard HEAD~1
```

When dealing with the ***non-fast-forward updates***:

```
git pull --rebase
```

This command replays the local changes on top of the fetched branch. For resolving *permission errors*, it is crucial to adjust the repository permissions or use sudo for elevated privileges when necessary.

Finally, *network issues* are common but can often be diagnosed by standard connectivity tools. Use ping and traceroute to ensure no disruptions between your machine and the remote repository. Verifying the configuration:

```
git config --global --list
```

These steps collectively address a broad range of common Git errors, providing practical solutions for an uninterrupted workflow.

9.3 Using Git Status and Git Log for Debugging

The git status and git log commands are essential tools for diagnosing and debugging issues within a Git repository. These commands provide detailed information about the current state of the repository and the history of changes, making it easier to identify and resolve problems.

git status is used to display the state of the working directory and the staging area. It allows the user to see which changes have been staged, which have not, and which files are not being tracked by Git. To use this command, simply execute:

```
git status
```

The output provides the following information:

- **Current Branch:** The branch that the user is currently working on.
- **Unstaged Changes:** Modifications in the working directory that have not yet been added to the staging area.
- **Staged Changes:** Modifications that have been added to the staging area and are ready to be committed.
- **Untracked Files:** Files that are not being tracked by Git.

Example output from git status:

```
On branch main
Your branch is up to date with 'origin/main'.

Changes to be committed:
  (use "git restore --staged <file>..." to unstage)
    modified:   example.txt

Changes not staged for commit:
  (use "git add <file>..." to update what will be committed)
  (use "git restore <file>..." to discard changes in working directory)
    modified:   another_example.txt

Untracked files:
  (use "git add <file>..." to include in what will be committed)
    new_file.txt
```

This output structure helps the user understand the repository's current state and identify any discrepancies in the staging process.

In contrast, git log is used to view the commit history of the repository. It displays a chronological list of commits and their associated metadata, such as author, date, and commit message. The basic syntax to invoke this command is:

```
git log
```

The default output of git log includes:

- **Commit Hash:** A unique identifier for the commit.
- **Author:** The name and email address of the individual who made the commit.
- **Date:** The timestamp of when the commit was made.
- **Commit Message:** A brief description of the changes introduced by the commit.

Example output from git log:

```
commit d6a8cd5f87e5837630e3ff3ef6715dadd4f6d9f2
Author: Jane Doe <jane.doe@example.com>
Date:   Mon Feb 21 14:22:58 2023 -0800

    Fix bug in sorting algorithm

commit ba7c1e5fa639ec4e65b3cfa4a9a4f6b7e8827f0e
Author: John Smith <john.smith@example.com>
Date:   Sun Feb 20 10:33:47 2023 -0800

    Add unit tests for new features
```

The verbosity of the git log command can be adjusted using various options:

- –oneline: Displays a condensed version of the commit history.
- –graph: Adds a graphical representation of the branch structure and merging history.
- –stat: Provides a summary of changes made in each commit, including the number of lines added and deleted.

Example of a condensed log with –oneline:

```
git log --oneline
```

```
d6a8cd5 Fix bug in sorting algorithm
ba7c1e5 Add unit tests for new features
```

Combining git status and git log provides a comprehensive understanding of the repository. While the former gives insight into the present content and configuration, the latter offers a detailed view of past changes and their evolution. Together, these commands help diagnose issues, trace the source of bugs, and understand the modifications that lead to the current state of the repository. Efficient use of these tools is integral for maintaining the repository's integrity and facilitating structured debugging and troubleshooting processes.

9.4 Resolving Merge Conflicts

Merge conflicts occur when changes from different branches cannot be automatically reconciled by Git. These conflicts typically arise when multiple changes to the same part of a file are made in separate branches that are then merged. Understanding the mechanism for identifying and resolving these conflicts is crucial for maintaining a streamlined workflow.

When performing a merge that leads to conflicts, Git will interrupt the merging process and prompt the user to manually resolve the conflicts. The conflicted files are clearly marked, allowing the user to identify which parts require reconciliation.

Upon encountering a merge conflict, Git modifies the conflicting files to include conflict markers. A typical conflict marker looks as follows:

```
<<<<<<< HEAD
content from the current branch
=======
content from the branch being merged
>>>>>>> branch_name
```

Here, the section between «««< HEAD and ======= represents the content from the current branch (the branch into which you are merging), while the section between ======= and »»»> branch_name shows the content from the branch that is being merged.

To resolve the conflict, the user must manually edit the file, choosing the appropriate content from each branch or creating a new combined version, then remove the conflict markers. After making the necessary changes, the file should look similar to this:

```
content from the current branch merged with content from the branch being merged
```

After manually resolving the conflicts in all affected files, the user must stage the resolved files using the git add command and complete the merge process by committing the changes:

```
git add filename
git commit
```

Git provides several tools to assist with resolving merge conflicts. One such utility is git mergetool, which launches a visual merge tool configured by the user (such as KDiff3 or Meld). This can be particularly useful for resolving complex conflicts. To use git mergetool, execute:

```
git mergetool
```

This command will open a graphical interface for each conflicted file, guiding the user through the resolution process. After resolving the conflict within the merge tool, the files will still need to be staged and committed as described earlier.

It is advisable to inspect the list of conflicted files before starting the resolution process. The command git status provides a summary of all files with conflicts, enabling the user to plan accordingly:

```
git status
```

Example output:

```
On branch master
You have unmerged paths.
  (fix conflicts and run "git commit")

Unmerged paths:
  (use "git add <file>..." to mark resolution)
        both modified:   example.txt

no changes added to commit (use "git add" and/or "git commit -a")
```

In situations where the conflict is difficult to resolve or the merge must be aborted, the merge process can be halted, and the working directory can be restored to its prior state using the following commands:

```
git merge --abort
```

The git merge –abort command reverts the repository to the state it was in before the merge attempt, discarding any changes made during the merge process. This action provides a safe fallback, allowing the user to rethink the approach or address potential conflicts separately.

It is beneficial to employ strategies that minimize the occurrence of conflicts. Regularly merging or rebasing changes from the main branch into feature branches can help keep changes synchronized and reduce the likelihood of significant conflicts. Additionally, clear communication within the team regarding file ownership and changes also plays a vital role in mitigating frequent conflicts.

Understanding and effectively managing merge conflicts are critical skills for any Git user, ensuring efficient collaboration and integrity of the codebase.

9.5 Recovering Lost Commits with Reflog

Git's reflog mechanism is an effective solution for recovering lost commits from a repository, offering a thorough record of every update reference that the repository has encountered. The reflog maintains logs of all the moves made to the tip of branches, making it an invaluable tool for Git users. This section provides an in-depth explanation of how to use the reflog to retrieve lost commits, ensuring clear guidance on practical applications.

When dealing with any situation of lost commits, the initial step is to examine the reflog. The reflog can be accessed using the following command:

```
git reflog
```

The output from this command displays a comprehensive list of all reference movements within the repository. For example:

```
1a2b3c4 (HEAD -> main) HEAD@{0}: commit: Updated CSS styles
4d5e6f7 HEAD@{1}: commit: Fixed bug in authentication
8g9h0i1 HEAD@{2}: commit: Added unit tests for login
2j3k4l5 HEAD@{3}: commit: Initial commit
```

Each line in the reflog output consists of the commit hash followed by the HEAD position at that instance and the action that triggered the new state. To retrieve a lost commit, identify the hash of the desired commit from this output.

Once the commit hash is identified, it can be restored to the working branch. Assume that the desired commit hash is 8g9h0i1 from the example above. To retrieve this commit, the 'git reset' or 'git checkout' commands can be utilized. If the goal is to permanently reset the branch to this lost commit, the following command should be used:

```
git reset --hard 8g9h0i1
```

This command will reset the current branch to the state of the commit 8g9h0i1, altering the working directory and staging area to match the state of that commit.

In situations where the objective is to create a new branch from the lost commit without altering the state of the current branch, the following command can instead be employed:

```
git checkout -b <new-branch-name> 8g9h0i1
```

This creates a new branch named *new-branch-name* from the commit 8g9h0i1. The working directory remains in the state of the current branch until the newly created branch is explicitly checked out.

Additionally, reflog can help when HEAD is mistakenly detached. In this state, your working directory is not on any branch, leading to the potential for commits to be lost upon moving away from the detached HEAD. The reflog can be used to identify and recover the commits made in this state. Consider the following command to visualize the recent HEAD positions:

```
git reflog show HEAD
```

This will provide a detailed history of HEAD movements, allowing identification of necessary commits.

To apply this, suppose a relevant commit hash is 3m4n5o6. One can create a new branch from this commit as follows:

```
git checkout -b <new-branch-name> 3m4n5o6
```

This action ensures that the commits are saved under a new branch name.

It is crucial to note that while the use of 'git reset –hard' is powerful for branch state restoration, it also entirely disposes of changes in the working directory and staging area that are not committed. Users should consider stashing changes or confirming that no critical modifications are pending before employing this command.

Employing 'git reflog' adeptly can save considerable effort, mitigating data loss risks and ensuring seamless recovery workflows for commits that may otherwise seem irretrievably lost.

9.6 Fixing Mistakes with Git Reset and Revert

In version control, mistakes can range from minor missteps to major errors that compromise the integrity of project timelines and data. Git provides powerful mechanisms like git reset and git revert to amend these errors effectively, maintaining the robustness of the repository.

Git Reset

The git reset command is a multifaceted tool that modifies the current branch's history to undo changes. It operates at three levels of granularity—soft, mixed, and hard—each of which corresponds to varying degrees of modification to the working directory, staging area (index), and commit history.

- A **soft** reset updates the head to the specified commit but leaves the staging area and working directory untouched. This is particularly useful when you need to adjust the last commit without altering the working state's contents.

  ```
  git reset --soft <commit_hash>
  ```

- A **mixed** reset, which is the default behavior if no flag is provided, updates the head and resets the staging area to match the specified commit, while leaving the working directory unchanged. This form is advantageous when you must unstage changes without modifying the actual file contents.

```
git reset --mixed <commit_hash>
```

- A **hard** reset updates the head, staging area, and working directory to match the specified commit. This action discards all changes, and thus, needs to be used with caution.

```
git reset --hard <commit_hash>
```

Usage Scenarios of Git Reset

To contextualize the use of git reset, let's consider a scenario where a developer accidentally commits sensitive information to the repository. Assume the accidental commit hash is c1d2e3f.

- **Using reset to amend the recent commit:** If the developer realizes the mistake immediately after the commit:

```
git reset --soft HEAD^
```

  This command moves the head to the previous commit while keeping the changes in the staging area, allowing the developer to edit and recommit correctly.

- **Unstaging files from a commit:** If a developer wants to unstage a file from the most recent commit:

```
git reset HEAD~1
```

  This shifts the head one commit back and unstages the changes for revising.

- **Discarding local changes completely:** For removing erroneous commits and local modifications:

```
git reset --hard origin/main
```

  Where origin/main represents the branch's desired safe state on the remote repository.

Git Revert

In contrast to git reset, which manipulates history, git revert constructs a new commit that inverses the changes of a specified commit. This approach is safer in collaborative environments since it preserves the historical chronology and ensures team members' repositories remain in sync.

```
git revert <commit_hash>
```

The process entails identifying the commit that introduced the undesired changes and applying the revert command to generate a new commit that nullifies those changes.

Usage Scenarios of Git Revert

To illustrate the usefulness of git revert, consider an accidental buggy commit identified by hash fa3b4cd.

- **Reverting a single commit:**

  ```
  git revert fa3b4cd
  ```

  This command opens a text editor to input the commit message for the revert operation, providing an opportunity to document the correction.

- **Reverting multiple commits:** If needing to undo a series of commits, specify the range and imply a sequential revert:

  ```
  git revert HEAD~2..HEAD
  ```

  Git processes each commit in the range inclusively, creating individual revert commits.

Understanding when to use git reset versus git revert hinges on the context and scope of the error. For single-user, local branches, git reset provides expedient and direct manipulation, whereas for collaborative projects, git revert ensures non-linear history remains intact and conflict-free. Each command plays a crucial role in maintaining clean, operational workflows and histories.

9.7 Handling Detached HEAD State

A detached HEAD state occurs in Git when the HEAD points to a commit directly rather than pointing to a branch. This situation is commonly encountered when you checkout a specific commit instead of a branch or use certain operations that place the HEAD at a specific commit. Understanding and effectively managing the detached HEAD state is critical to avoiding confusion and potential data loss.

To identify if you are in a detached HEAD state, one of the simplest approaches is to inspect the output of the git status command. In a detached HEAD state, the status output will indicate that you are not on any branch:

```
$ git status
HEAD detached at <commit_SHA1>
nothing to commit, working tree clean
```

When the HEAD is detached, any commits you make will not be associated with the current branch. Instead, these commits will hang off the commit that was checked out. If you switch to another branch without taking action, the commits made in the detached HEAD state may become unreachable and could be eventually lost when Git performs garbage collection.

To exit the detached HEAD state and attach the HEAD back to a branch, you can use the git checkout command. For instance, to switch to the master branch:

```
$ git checkout master
```

However, in cases where you have made commits in the detached HEAD state that you want to preserve, you need to integrate these commits into an existing branch. This can be done through various methods such as creating a new branch from the current detached HEAD or merging the commits into another branch.

One common approach is to create a new branch from the current commit:

```
$ git checkout -b <new-branch-name>
```

This command creates a new branch with a specified name starting from the current commit, effectively preserving the commits made in the detached HEAD state. Alternatively, if you intend to attach these commits to an existing branch, you can switch to the target branch and merge the detached commits. For example:

```
$ git checkout master
$ git merge <detached-HEAD-SHA1>
```

If you only need to incorporate a single commit or a few commits from the detached state, git cherry-pick can be an optimal solution:

```
$ git checkout master
$ git cherry-pick <commit_SHA1>
```

The cherry-pick command applies the specified commit onto the current branch, allowing selective inclusion of changes.

Consider a scenario where you've accidentally found yourself in a detached HEAD state after checking out a previous commit for review or testing:

```
$ git checkout abcdef1234
Note: checking out 'abcdef1234'.

You are in 'detached HEAD' state. You can look around, make experimental
changes and commit them, and you can discard any commits you make in this
state without impacting any branches by switching back to a branch.

...
```

In this situation, if you decide to keep the changes, you can create a new branch:

```
$ git checkout -b feature-branch
Switched to a new branch 'feature-branch'
```

Alternatively, if you determine the changes are experimental and no longer needed, you can simply checkout the intended branch:

```
$ git checkout master
```

It is essential to grasp the implications and nuances of operating in a detached HEAD state to ensure that pivotal changes are not inadvertently lost. By following the careful practices outlined above, you can navigate this state effectively and maintain the robustness of your Git workflows.

9.8 Debugging with Git Bisect

git bisect is an essential tool for diagnosing and pinpointing the introduction of bugs within a repository's history. It automates the binary search process, efficiently isolating the commit that introduced a malfunction. The command operates by iteratively checking out commits, bisecting the commit history, and allowing the user to indicate whether the current commit is *good* or *bad*. By systematically narrowing down the range of potential problem commits, git bisect facilitates the identification of the offending change.

Initiating a bisect session begins with the command:

```
git bisect start
```

Next, you must identify a *bad* commit, which refers to a state where the bug is present. This is done using:

```
git bisect bad <commit>
```

Here, <commit> specifies the SHA-1 hash of the bad commit, or a branch/tag that points to it. For example, if the bug exists in the latest commit, HEAD can be used in place of <commit>:

```
git bisect bad HEAD
```

The next step requires specifying a *good* commit, a state where the bug was not present. This is indicated with:

```
git bisect good <commit>
```

With both *good* and *bad* commits identified, Git proceeds with the bisect process. It checks out commits halfway between the known good and bad points, guiding the user to test each one. The user then determines whether each checked-out commit represents a good state or a bad state. Based on the user's input, Git narrows down the range until the problematic commit is isolated.

Example: Consider a scenario where a bug is identified, and the current commit is labeled as *bad*:

```
git bisect start
git bisect bad HEAD
git bisect good v1.2
```

Git responds by checking out a commit approximately halfway between HEAD and v1.2. Suppose git bisect checks out commit abc1234. You test this commit and determine it is *good*. Inform Git using:

```
git bisect good abc1234
```

Git will continue to bisect the remaining range. If the next commit checked out (e.g., def5678) is *bad*, the user issues:

```
git bisect bad def5678
```

This iterative process continues until only one commit remains. Git will then display the commit that introduced the bug. Example output:

```
def5678 is the first bad commit
commit def5678
Author: Developer <developer@example.com>
Date:   yyyy-mm-dd

    Introduced unexpected behavior

:040000 040000 fbc6f9d 0a878e1 M      myfile.c
```

To conclude the bisect session, use:

```
git bisect reset
```

This command restores the working directory to its original HEAD, ending the bisect session. This process is highly efficient in a large repository where manually inspecting each commit would be impractical.

In conjunction with automated testing, git bisect can be further streamlined. Automatized scripts can be used to test each commit within the bisect process, relieving the user from manually determining the state:

```
git bisect run <script>
```

Here, <script> is an executable that returns 0 for *good* commits and a non-zero status for *bad* commits. Implementing such automation significantly reduces the time and effort required in debugging.

Considerations when using git bisect include ensuring a clean workspace and understanding the context of intermediate commits, which may not be functional on their own due to the nature of development work. Nonetheless, git bisect remains an invaluable tool in the diagnostic arsenal, providing a straightforward and effective method to uncover the source of bugs within the commit history, ultimately aiding in robust software maintenance and development.

9.9 Restoring Deleted Branches

Branches in Git provide a mechanism for parallel development by allowing separate lines of work within a repository. Occasionally, a branch may be deleted accidentally or prematurely, leading to a requirement to restore it to recover valuable work. Git provides several methods to restore deleted branches, leveraging concepts of commits, reflogs, and reference pointers.

Using Reflog to Restore Deleted Branches

The most reliable method to restore a deleted branch in Git is by utilizing the reflog, which records all movements of the HEAD and branches in the repository. The reflog maintains a history of changes, including deletions, making it straightforward to find the commit to which the deleted branch was pointing.

First, use the following command to list the reflog:

```
git reflog
```

This command outputs a list of actions that have moved the HEAD pointer. Each entry will have an identifier (e.g., ‘HEAD@number‘), the commit hash, and a description of the action. Locate the commit hash corresponding to the last state of the deleted branch before deletion.

Assuming the commit hash is ‘abc1234‘, the branch can be restored by creating a new branch at that commit:

```
git branch <branch_name> abc1234
```

Replace <branch_name> with the intended name for the restored branch. This command creates a new branch at the point where the original branch was deleted.

Using Git Log to Find the Commit Hash

If reflog information is insufficient or unavailable, the git log command can help find the commit relatively easily. Execute:

```
git log --all --graph --oneline --decorate
```

This command provides a visual representation of the commit history, enabling identification of the lost branch by inspecting commit messages, dates, and decorations. Once the appropriate commit hash is identified, the branch can be recreated using the same method as with the reflog:

```
git branch <branch_name> <commit_hash>
```

Tips for Preventing Accidental Branch Deletion

Preventing accidental deletion is key. Employ techniques such as:

- Protected Branches: Configure Git to avoid deletions in critical branches.
- Prevention Hooks: Implement server-side hooks that prevent deletion without confirmation or specific permissions.
- Regular Backups: Regularly back up the repository to another

server or storage medium.

Adding these precautions helps ensure that branches are not deleted without careful consideration and necessary verification steps.

Example output of 'git reflog':

```
377b88f (HEAD -> master) HEAD@{0}: commit: Update documentation
a7d3c1e HEAD@{1}: commit: Add new feature
85c85d0 (old-branch) HEAD@{2}: branch: Deleted branch old-branch (was abc1234)
abc1234 HEAD@{3}: commit: Initial commit for old-branch
```

In this example, commit 'abc1234' is the target for restoring 'old-branch'. Running 'git branch old-branch abc1234' reestablishes it.

Efficient branch restoration demands familiarity with Git's internal mechanisms for commit history and branch references. Mastery over these tools ensures that no work is irrevocably lost, thereby maintaining a robust development workflow.

9.10 Checking and Repairing Repository Integrity

Ensuring the integrity of a Git repository is crucial for maintaining a reliable and functional version control environment. Git provides several commands to verify and repair the integrity of a repository. This section delves into these mechanisms, emphasizing the importance of routine checks, common integrity issues, and how to resolve them systematically.

To verify the integrity of your repository, you can use the command:

```
git fsck
```

The git fsck command (which stands for file system consistency check) inspects the repository for various integrity issues. It reports any object corruption, misplaced objects, and other filesystem-level errors.

An example of typical git fsck output is shown below:

```
Checking object directories: 100% (256/256), done.
Checking objects: 100% (228/228), done.
dangling blob 3f6b8345b5d1a208eb45b3bd2c2a8574c471c5c5
dangling commit 40f775ec5029cad7e9b0638a9c5fd770c0f68e05
broken link from tree 693d8b8b5b1a18dedc1508a8d96a1a2c13673572
             to blob 9da3e4fa91a0d03ba40c0c564a8b48cb19eeded5
missing commit c59d1b40d7a7e6d7e041da041241d7a476f9c132
```

The example output presents different types of integrity issues such as dangling blobs and commits, broken links, and missing commits.

- **Dangling Objects**: These are objects that are not reachable from any reference, typically because they have been orphaned by subsequent commits. Dangling objects are not inherently problematic but may signify unmerged changes or lost work.
- **Broken Links**: These occur when a tree object references a non-existent blob. This can result from premature garbage collection or file corruption.
- **Missing Commits**: This indicates that a commit object referenced by other objects is missing, which can severely impact the repository's history integrity.

Repairing the Repository

- **Dangling Objects**

  If dangling commits or blobs are reported, you may inspect them further to determine their relevance. You can use:

  ```
  git show <object_id>
  ```

  If you determine that the dangling objects contain valuable data that should not be discarded, consider creating a new branch from the dangling commit or incorporating the changes manually into the current branch.

- **Broken Links and Missing Objects**

  Broken links and missing objects are more serious as they indicate a loss of repository history or data corruption. You can attempt reconstruction by first identifying a clean, recent backup of the repository. If such backups are not available, you can try the following:

  - **Reflog**: Use the reflog to identify references to past states before the corruption occurred.

    ```
    git reflog
    ```

    The reflog provides a chronological history of where your HEAD and branch references have pointed to in the past, allowing you to recover specific commits.

- **Fetch from Remote**: If the local repository is corrupted and a remote repository is considered healthy, fetching and resetting to the remote state is a viable option.

```
git fetch origin
git reset --hard origin/main
```

  This sequence ensures that the local repository aligns with the state of the remote repository, thereby discarding local corruptions.

- **Bitwise Comparison with Remote**: For a thorough verification, you can compare your repository with a known-good remote repository using bitwise comparison of objects:

```
git clone --mirror <repository_url> /tmp/repo-mirror
cd /path/to/local/repo
git fetch --all
git fsck --full
```

  This process ensures a full verification against the remote, highlighting any discrepancies between the local and remote repositories.

Ensuring repository integrity is essential for maintaining reliable version control and avoiding catastrophic data loss. Regular use of git fsck, combined with diligent backup strategies, ensures that your development workflow remains robust and your repository data intact.

Chapter 10

Best Practices and Tips

This chapter outlines best practices and tips for using Git effectively. It covers writing clear commit messages, employing strategic branching methods, and maintaining a clean commit history. Additionally, it discusses conducting effective code reviews, managing large repositories, and implementing secure Git practices. The chapter also explores the use of Git aliases for improved efficiency, the importance of documentation, and staying updated with the latest Git features and updates.

10.1 Introduction to Git Best Practices

Git is a powerful tool for version control, offering the flexibility and robustness needed for efficient code management. To leverage its full potential, adherence to established best practices is essential. This section delves into various practices aimed at optimizing Git's functionalities, ensuring not only a streamlined workflow but also the maintainability and integrity of the repository.

Consistent Commit Messages: Writing clear and meaningful commit messages is crucial. These messages serve as a historical record and allow collaborators to understand the rationale behind changes quickly. A succinct format is generally followed:

```
<Subject Line>
<Blank Line>
<Body>
```

The subject line should be a brief summary of the changes (50 characters or fewer), followed by an optional body that provides context or details, especially for complex commits.

Strategic Branching: Adoption of a branching strategy such as Git Flow, GitHub Flow, or Trunk-Based Development significantly impacts the efficiency of parallel development processes.

- **Git Flow:** Utilizes multiple branches (e.g., 'master', 'develop', 'feature', 'release', 'hotfix') to manage various stages of development and production code.
- **GitHub Flow:** A simpler approach with only 'master' and 'feature' branches, suitable for continuous delivery environments.
- **Trunk-Based Development:** Focuses on a single 'main' branch where all developers integrate small changes frequently, reducing complex merges and integration issues.

Atomic Commits: Ensuring that each commit embodies a single logical change facilitates easier code reviews and problem isolation. This means avoiding commits that encompass multiple unrelated changes.

Descriptive Branch Names: Branch names should convey the purpose or scope of the branch clearly. Following a naming convention aids in managing branches effectively. Examples of useful naming conventions include:

```
feature/<description>
bugfix/<description>
hotfix/<description>
release/<version>
```

Regular Merges and Rebases: Regularly merging or rebasing feature branches with 'develop' or 'master' helps to minimize merge conflicts and ensures that changes are integrated smoothly. While merging retains complete history, rebasing creates a linear history, which can be advantageous for keeping the commit log clean but requires careful handling to avoid rewriting public history.

Code Reviews: Conduct formal code reviews through pull requests (PRs) to maintain code quality and encourage knowledge sharing. A standard PR should:

- Include a description of changes.

- Reference any relevant issue numbers.

- Provide any necessary context or screenshots.

Reviewers should scan for potential bugs, adherence to coding standards, and clarity in logic, ensuring the overall quality of the codebase remains high.

Avoiding Committed Secrets: Maintain repository security by avoiding the inclusion of sensitive data (e.g., passwords, API keys) in commits. Utilize '.gitignore' to exclude files that might contain such information and consider using tools like 'git-secrets' to scan for secrets before committing.

Utilizing Git Hooks: Git hooks are scripts that run automatically at specific points in the Git workflow. Pre-commit hooks, for example, can automate tasks such as code formatting, linting, and running tests, ensuring that only code meeting predefined quality criteria is committed. Here's an implementation of a simple Git pre-commit hook:

```
#!/bin/sh
# Pre-commit hook to check for code formatting
if ! ./run_formatter.sh; then
    echo "Code is not formatted properly. Please format your code."
    exit 1
fi
```

Documentation: Regularly update both code comments and README files to reflect the current state of the repository. Comprehensive documentation aids new developers in understanding the project architecture and workflow.

Regular Repository Maintenance: Perform regular housekeeping activities such as pruning obsolete branches and rebasing before merging long-lived branches. This keeps the repository clean and avoids unnecessary bloat.

By ingraining these best practices into the daily workflow, teams can enhance the collaborative development experience, reduce the likelihood of errors, and maintain a high-quality codebase. Committing to these guidelines fosters a more organized, efficient, and secure working environment in any Git-based project.

10.2 Writing Good Commit Messages

Commit messages serve as a vital form of documentation that conveys the purpose and context of changes made to a repository. They aid in understanding the evolution of the codebase, facilitating code reviews, debugging, and future maintenance. High-quality commit messages can significantly enhance the collaboration and maintainability of a project.

A well-structured commit message typically consists of a summary line, sometimes followed by a detailed description. The summary line should be concise, ideally no more than 50 characters, and clearly state what the commit does. If additional context is necessary, it can be provided in the body of the message, which should be wrapped at 72 characters per line for readability.

```
Fix issue with user login authentication

The authentication module was failing to validate the user when
special characters were present in the password. This commit fixes
the issue by updating the regex pattern used in the authentication
function.

Fixes: #123
```

In the example above, the summary line succinctly describes the change, while the detailed description offers context and references the issue it addresses. It's essential to follow these practices to ensure commit messages are informative and useful:

- **Start with a Capital Letter**
  Begin the summary line with a capital letter. It respects the sentence case convention, enhancing readability and professionalism.

- **Use the Imperative Mood**
  The imperative mood is standard for commit messages, as it elicits the command required to apply the commit. For instance, "Fix login bug" instead of "Fixed login bug".

- **Be Concise Yet Descriptive**
  Your commit message should be brief but sufficient to understand the change. Avoid unnecessary words but provide adequate detail to grasp the modification's intent.

- **Separate Subject from Body with a Blank Line**
  If your commit message requires a detailed description, ensure

there is a blank line separating the summary from the body. This separation makes the message more readable and allows tools like git log to parse them correctly.

```
Change the primary color scheme

This change aligns our application with the company's new branding
guidelines. The primary color was updated from blue to green.
```

- **Explain the What and Why, Not the How**
  Focus on what changes have been made and why they were necessary, rather than how they were applied. The diff already shows the how, so the commit message should provide the reasoning behind the change.

- **Reference Issues and Reviewers**
  When applicable, reference related issues or pull requests and mention any reviewers or collaborators involved in the change. This adds traceability and acknowledges contributions.

```
Add feature to export user data as CSV

Allows users to export their profile data in CSV format. This feature
is essential for users needing offline data handling.
Reviewers: @alice, @bob
Related: #456, #789
```

- **Use ‘Fixes‘ or ‘Closes‘ for Issue References**
  When a commit resolves an issue, include keywords like ‘Fixes‘, ‘Closes‘, followed by the issue number. This practice automatically closes the issue when the commit is merged.

- **Incremental and Atomic Commits**
  Ensure each commit is an atomic unit of change—only one distinct change per commit. This granularity supports better rollback capabilities and a clear project history.

- **Review Commit Messages**
  Before finalizing a commit, review the message for clarity, completeness, and correctness. Consistent and well-considered commit messages contribute to a manageable and understandable project history, facilitating future team collaboration and project evolution.

Implementing these guidelines will lead to more meaningful and navigable commit histories, ultimately benefiting all contributors in a collaborative coding environment.

10.3 Branching Strategies

Effective branching strategies are fundamental for managing code development with Git. Proper branching facilitates organized development workflows, allowing team members to work independently on different features or bug fixes while ensuring a cohesive codebase. This section delves into several widely-adopted branching strategies, detailing their workflows and benefits.

One of the most popular strategies is *Git Flow*, which introduces a strict branching model designed around the project release cycle. Git Flow defines two main branches:

- **main**: This branch contains production-ready code. Every commit to this branch should be deployable.
- **develop**: This is the integration branch for features. It serves as an aggregation point for completed features before they are merged into the *main* branch.

In addition to these main branches, Git Flow includes several supporting branches:

- **feature branches**: These branches are derived from *develop* and are used to develop new features. When a feature is complete, the branch is merged back into *develop*.
- **release branches**: Once *develop* has attained a state deemed sufficient for a release, a *release* branch is created from *develop*. This branch allows for minor bug fixes and other release-related activities before it is merged into *main* and *develop*.
- **hotfix branches**: These branches are created from *main* when an urgent fix is required in the production environment. After the fix is completed, the branch is merged into both *main* and *develop*.

Another common strategy is the *GitHub Flow*, known for its simplicity and efficiency. GitHub Flow involves the following steps:

- Create a new branch from *main* for each new feature or fix.
- Make commits to this branch as work progresses. Each commit should represent a logical unit of work.
- Use pull requests to solicit feedback and conduct code reviews. This process ensures that code changes are examined before being integrated.
- Once the feature or fix is complete and reviewed, merge the branch back into *main*.
- Deploy the code from *main*.

GitHub Flow provides continuous integration, promoting a culture where code is always deployable and continuously improved through iterative development and frequent reviews.

GitLab Flow is another branching strategy that expands on GitHub Flow by introducing the concept of *environments* and *release branches*. It supports different deployment environments, such as staging, pre-production, and production. The strategy involves:

- Developers create feature branches from the *main* branch for each feature or fix.
- Once a feature is complete, the feature branch is merged into an *environment branch* (e.g., *staging*).
- Changes are tested in the staging environment. Bug fixes are integrated into the staging branch until the code is deemed ready for production.
- Approved changes from the staging branch are then merged into a *release branch* or directly into *main* for deployment.

This strategy facilitates the process of moving code through various stages of testing and quality assurance before reaching the production environment.

An alternative approach, *Trunk-Based Development*, eschews long-lived branches in favor of frequent integration into a *main* branch. This approach promotes continuous integration and delivery (CI/CD), characterized by:

- Developers work on short-lived branches or commit directly to the *main* branch.
- Code changes are integrated continuously, with comprehensive automated testing to ensure stability.
- Feature flags or toggles may be used to enable or disable new features dynamically without requiring long-lived branches.

Trunk-Based Development enhances transparency and ensures that the codebase always represents the latest development state, allowing for rapid releases and minimal merge conflicts.

Each branching strategy presents distinct advantages and potential challenges. The choice of strategy should align with team size, project scope, deployment frequency, and organizational practices. Proper implementation and adherence to the chosen branching model enrich the version control process, elevate code quality, and smooth the path toward consistent, reliable releases.

10.4 Keeping a Clean Commit History

A clean commit history is essential for maintaining a manageable and comprehensible project repository, facilitating better collaboration and troubleshooting. This section will delve into practical methods for achieving and maintaining a clean commit history.

Atomic Commits: Each commit should encapsulate a single logical change, making it easier to understand and review. Avoid bundling multiple unrelated modifications within a single commit. Before staging changes, consider the scope of each logical change.

```
# Staging changes related to feature A
git add featureA_file1.py featureA_file2.py
git commit -m "Implement feature A for user authentication"

# Staging changes related to bugfix B
git add bugfixB_file3.js
git commit -m "Fix bug B related to input validation in the frontend"
```

Meaningful Commit Messages: Clear and descriptive commit messages aid in understanding the intent behind changes. A rigorous convention, such as starting the message with a relevant keyword, can be helpful. For instance, use "Fix:", "Add:", "Refactor:", etc.

```
Refactor: Improve the readability of the data processing module
Fix: Resolve issue with null pointer exception in user registration
Docs: Update API documentation for the latest endpoints
```

Interactive Rebase: Use git rebase -i to clean up your commit history before integrating changes into the main branch. This interactive mode allows you to reorder, squash, or edit commits for a cleaner history.

```
# Launch interactive rebase for the last 5 commits
git rebase -i HEAD~5
```

In the rebase editor, you can mark commits with commands such as pick, reword, squash, and fixup. For instance:

```
pick 123abc7 Implement feature A for user authentication
reword 234bcd8 Ensure proper password hashing
squash 345cde9 Fix typo in password hashing function
```

Amending Commits: If you need to change the most recent commit, use git commit –amend to include additional changes or improve the commit message. This keeps the history concise and prevents unnecessary commits.

```
# Make changes and stage them
git add modified_file.py

# Amend the previous commit
git commit --amend -m "Refactor: Modify user authentication logic"
```

Avoiding Redundant Commits: Ensure that you do not repeatedly commit trivial changes. Use tools like git diff and git status to review modifications before committing to avoid cluttering the history with unnecessary entries.

```
# Check for modifications
git status

# Review differences
git diff

# Commit only necessary changes
git add necessary_file.py
git commit -m "Enhance logging for user authentication flow"
```

Merge Commits: While merging branches, consider using the –no-ff flag to enforce non-fast-forward merges, ensuring that all merges appear in the commit history. This helps in preserving the contextual information about the feature branches.

```
# Merge the feature branch into main with a merge commit
git checkout main
git merge --no-ff feature-branch -m "Merge feature-branch with user authentication
```

```
improvements"
```

A clean commit history significantly improves the ease of navigation within a repository. By adopting these practices, one can facilitate better code reviews, debugging processes, and overall code maintainability.

10.5 Effective Code Reviews

Code reviews serve as a critical practice in modern software development processes. This section elaborates on the importance, techniques, and tools essential for conducting efficient and effective code reviews, ensuring the consistent quality and maintainability of the codebase.

The primary goal of code reviews is to identify and rectify potential issues in the codebase, facilitate knowledge sharing among team members, and uphold coding standards. An effective code review process can significantly enhance the overall quality of the software project, leading to more robust and secure applications.

It is essential to approach code reviews with a structured and collaborative mindset. Here are some key practices for conducting effective code reviews:

- **Establish Clear Guidelines:** Define and document coding standards and guidelines that the team should adhere to. This includes formatting conventions, naming conventions, architectural patterns, and best practices. Providing a checklist can help reviewers ensure all aspects are covered consistently.

  ```
  Example Checklist:
  - Adherence to coding standards
  - Proper error handling
  - Security considerations
  - Efficiency and performance
  - Readability and maintainability
  - Logical coherence
  - Adequate testing
  ```

- **Use Automated Tools:** Leverage automated tools and static analysis to catch common issues before the code reaches the review stage. These tools can enforce coding standards, detect potential bugs, and identify security vulnerabilities.

  ```
  $ git pre-commit run -a # Run all pre-commit hooks
  ```

```
$ eslint src/ # Run ESLint for JavaScript/TypeScript
$ flake8 . # Python linting
$ pmd-bin/bin/run.sh pmd -d . -R rulesets/java/quickstart.xml -f text
```

- **Provide Constructive Feedback:** Comments during code reviews should be clear, concise, and constructive. Highlight what has been done well as well as suggesting improvements. Aim to foster a collaborative environment rather than a critical one. Use precise language explaining why a change is needed.

```
Example of Constructive Feedback:
- Positive: "Good use of descriptive variable names, which improves readability."
- Suggestive: "Consider using a list comprehension here to make this loop more concise."
- Clarifying: "Can you explain why we chose this particular algorithm? Are there alternatives?"
```

- **Limit the Scope:** Code reviews are more effective when they are focused on small, manageable changes. Large pull requests can be overwhelming and more challenging to review thoroughly. Encourage frequent, smaller commits to facilitate easier reviews.

- **Prioritize High-Risk Changes:** Focus more attention on changes that have higher risk or impact, such as modifications to critical sections of the codebase, complex algorithms, or security-sensitive areas. Ensuring that these parts are thoroughly reviewed can prevent significant issues in the future.

- **Ensure Participation from All Team Members:** Involve multiple team members in the code review process to promote diverse perspectives and knowledge sharing. Rotate the review responsibilities to avoid bottlenecks and ensure that knowledge is not siloed with specific individuals.

- **Continuous Improvement:** Regularly review and refine the code review process itself. Gather feedback from team members on what works well and what can be improved. Adapting the process based on this feedback will help in achieving better results over time.

- **Use Version Control Features:** Make use of version control features that facilitate code reviews, such as pull requests and inline comments on platforms like GitHub, GitLab, and Bitbucket. These platforms provide integrated review tools that streamline the process.

```
Example GitHub Pull Request Workflow:
1. Developer pushes changes to a feature branch.
2. Create a pull request (PR) targeting the main branch.
3. Automated tests and linting run on PR creation.
4. Reviewers provide feedback and request changes.
5. Developer addresses feedback and updates the PR.
6. Reviewers approve changes.
7. Merge PR into the main branch after all checks pass.
```

- **Acknowledge Good Practices:** Recognizing and acknowledging good practices and improvements during code reviews encourages positive reinforcement and motivates developers to maintain high standards continually.
- **Balance Between Rigidity and Flexibility:** While it is essential to enforce coding standards, sometimes there might be valid reasons to deviate from established guidelines. Maintain a balance between rigour and flexibility to accommodate innovative solutions or performance optimizations.

By adhering to these practices, teams can conduct more effective code reviews that not only improve code quality but also foster a culture of collaboration and continuous improvement. Effective code reviews are an investment in the long-term health and success of a software project.

10.6 Managing Large Repositories

Effective management of large repositories in Git requires addressing specific challenges such as long clone times, increased storage requirements, and potentially cumbersome operations. Understanding and implementing strategies to mitigate these issues can lead to a more efficient and maintainable repository.

Repositories tend to grow in size due to the accumulation of various elements such as large binary files, lengthy commit histories, and extensive branching. Tools like Git LFS (Large File Storage) and techniques like shallow cloning are essential for managing repository size.

Git Large File Storage (LFS): Git LFS is an extension that helps manage large files by replacing them with text pointers inside Git, while storing the actual file contents on a remote server. This method reduces the size of the main repository.

To install Git LFS:

```
git lfs install
```

To track files using Git LFS, specify the file types you want to handle:

```
git lfs track "*.psd"
git add .gitattributes
git commit -m "track PSD files with LFS"
```

This configuration ensures that subsequent additions of specified file types will be managed by Git LFS.

Shallow Cloning: Shallow cloning fetches a repository's history only to a specified depth. This method is particularly useful when you only need the latest state of the repository and not the entire history, significantly reducing the clone time and disk usage.

To clone a repository to a depth of one commit:

```
git clone --depth 1 <repository-url>
```

For already cloned repositories, the history can be truncated:

```
git fetch --depth 1
git prune
```

Split Large Repositories: Monolithic repositories can become unwieldy over time. Splitting such repositories into smaller, more manageable ones can enhance maintainability and performance. This practice involves segregating different components or projects into individual repositories, which can then be incorporated into the primary repository using submodules or tools like Git Subtree.

Setting up a submodule:

```
git submodule add <repository-url> <path-to-submodule>
git commit -m "Add submodule"
```

Updating submodules requires specific pull commands:

```
git submodule update --remote
```

Repository Optimization: Periodically, it is useful to optimize the repository to remove unnecessary files, compress data, and improve performance. Git provides several commands to assist with this.

Cleaning up unnecessary files:

```
git gc --prune=now --aggressive
```

This command will garbage collect and optimize the repository, which can be scheduled regularly as part of repository maintenance.

Optimal Branching and Tagging: Efficient use of branching and tagging helps reduce bloat and keeps the repository clean. Long-living branches should be limited, and old branches that aren't needed should be pruned regularly.

To delete a local branch:

```
git branch -d <branch-name>
```

To delete a remote branch:

```
git push origin --delete <branch-name>
```

Tags offer a lightweight way to mark important commits without the overhead associated with branches. To create a tag:

```
git tag -a v1.0 -m "Version 1.0"
git push origin --tags
```

Monitoring Repository Size: Regular monitoring of the repository's size can preempt management issues. Tools like GitHub's repository analytics and CLI commands can provide insights into repository growth patterns.

To list the size of each object in the repository:

```
git count-objects -vH
```

Monitoring and optimizing large repositories are ongoing processes that involve regular checks and maintenance actions. Proper configuration of commits, branches, and files can ensure the repository remains efficient and manageable. By implementing these best practices, large repositories can be as effective and swift as smaller ones.

10.7 Secure Git Practices

When practicing version control with Git, it is imperative to integrate robust security measures to safeguard code integrity, confidentiality, and authenticity. This section delves into key practices that enhance the security of Git repositories, ranging from access control to cryptographic measures.

- **Access Control and Authentication**

  Ensuring that only authorized individuals have access to the repository is a primary step. Git supports several authentication mechanisms including SSH keys, HTTPS with username and password, and personal access tokens. The most secure and recommended method involves using SSH keys.

To generate an SSH key pair, use the following command:

```
$ ssh-keygen -t rsa -b 4096 -C "your_email@example.com"
```

This command generates a 4096-bit RSA key pair, which can be securely added to your Git service provider account (e.g., GitHub, GitLab). Always use strong and unique passwords for your accounts and employ multi-factor authentication (MFA) when possible.

- **Secure Communication with GitHub, GitLab, and Similar Services**

  When using Git over HTTPS, ensure that SSL/TLS is enabled to encrypt the communication between your local machine and the server. Most modern Git hosting services enforce HTTPS by default. Verifying the authenticity of the host by checking the SSL certificates helps prevent man-in-the-middle attacks.

- **Protecting Sensitive Data**

  Be vigilant in ensuring that sensitive data such as passwords, API keys, and secret tokens are not inadvertently committed into the repository. Utilize .gitignore files to exclude such sensitive files:

```
# .gitignore example to exclude sensitive data
*.env
*.key
*.pem
*.config
```

  If sensitive data has already been committed, tools like BFG Repo-Cleaner or Git's built-in filter-branch command can be used to purge this data from history.

```
$ bfg --delete-files "*.key"
$ git filter-branch --force --index-filter \
  "git rm --cached --ignore-unmatch *.key" \
  --prune-empty --tag-name-filter cat -- --all
```

- **Signing Commits and Tags**

  Signing commits and tags with GPG (GNU Privacy Guard) provides cryptographic assurance of the author's identity. This helps in authenticating that the code changes are indeed made by a trusted individual.

To sign a commit, first ensure you have a GPG key configured:

```
$ gpg --gen-key
$ git config --global user.signingkey <GPG_KEY_ID>
```

Sign commits using the -S flag:

```
$ git commit -S -m "Signed commit message"
```

Verify signed commits with:

```
$ git log --show-signature
```

- **Monitoring and Auditing Repositories**

  Continuous monitoring and regular auditing are crucial in maintaining repository security. Tools like Git hooks can be employed to enforce security policies at various stages (pre-commit, pre-push). For example, a pre-commit hook to scan for sensitive information can be created in the .git/hooks/pre-commit file:

```
#!/bin/sh
# Detect potential sensitive data leaks
if grep -r '[A-Za-z0-9_/]+=+' . ; then
  echo "Sensitive data detected. Aborting commit."
  exit 1
fi
```

  In addition, using third-party services such as GitGuardian, which offer automated scanning for secrets in your repositories, can enhance your overall security posture.

- **Regularly Update Git and Dependencies**

  Keeping Git and all related tools up to date is necessary to protect against vulnerabilities. Install updates promptly and follow security advisories from trusted sources. For example, using a package manager:

```
$ sudo apt-get update
$ sudo apt-get install git
```

- **Educating Team Members**

  Finally, fostering a security-aware culture within the team is critical. Regular training on secure coding practices, the importance of code review processes, and staying informed about the latest security threats can substantially reduce risks. Conduct periodic security-focused code reviews and cultivate a proactive approach to identifying and mitigating potential security concerns.

Integrating these practices into your Git workflow will significantly mitigate security risks and protect your valuable codebase from potential threats.

10.8 Using Git Aliases for Efficiency

Git aliases serve as a powerful mechanism to enhance efficiency and streamline workflows by allowing users to define shortcuts for commonly used Git commands. This customization feature reduces keystrokes and minimizes the potential for repetitive command typos.

To create a Git alias, use the following format:

```
git config --global alias.<alias_name> '<git_command>'
```

For example, to create a shortcut for the 'git status' command, you might define an alias as follows:

```
git config --global alias.st 'status'
```

After this configuration, executing 'git st' in the terminal will be equivalent to running 'git status', displaying the repository's status efficiently.

Example Aliases and their Applications

- **Status Check**:

  ```
  git config --global alias.s 'status -s'
  ```

  This alias provides a compact status output with 'git s', using the short format option '-s'.

- **Log Viewing**:

  ```
  git config --global alias.lg 'log --oneline --graph --decorate --all'
  ```

  By using 'git lg', users can view a streamlined, visually represented log of commits.

- **Adding to Stage**:

  ```
  git config --global alias.a 'add .'
  ```

This alias allows for quick additions of all changes in the working directory to the staging area with 'git a'.

- **Commit with Message**:

```
git config --global alias.cm 'commit -m'
```

Simplifying the commit process by using 'git cm 'message''.

- **Displaying Branches**:

```
git config --global alias.br 'branch'
```

This allows users to list all branches quickly by typing 'git br'.

- **Fetching and Pruning**:

```
git config --global alias.fp 'fetch --prune'
```

This alias combines fetching and pruning of remote-tracking branches with a single 'git fp' command.

Grouping Multiple Commands

Git aliases can also group multiple commands to automate repetitive tasks. For instance, combining fetching the latest changes and displaying the log:

```
git config --global alias.sync '!git fetch && git pull --rebase'
```

This alias named 'sync' first fetches the latest changes from the remote repository and then rebases the current branch to integrate those changes, all triggered by 'git sync'.

Using Scripts within Aliases

Aliases can execute scripts, expanding their power considerably. For complex sequences:

```
git config --global alias.cleanup '!f() { git fetch --prune && git branch -vv | grep ": gone
    ]" | awk '"'"'{print $1}'"'"' | xargs git branch -d; }; f'
```

This 'cleanup' alias fetches remote changes, prunes stale branches, and deletes local branches that are tracking deleted remote branches.

Viewing and Modifying Existing Aliases

To view existing aliases:

```
git config --get-regexp alias
```

This command lists all defined Git aliases, elucidating predefined shortcuts. To remove an alias:

```
git config --global --unset alias.<alias_name>
```

Finally, aliases significantly reduce typing overhead and streamline the workflow of complex command sequences in Git, promoting higher productivity and fewer command input errors.

10.9 Documentation and Maintaining Repositories

Documentation is a cornerstone of effective project management and collaboration within software development. Proper documentation ensures that team members, whether current or future, can understand the project's state and functionality, thus facilitating smoother transitions and ongoing development.

A comprehensive Git repository should include several types of documentation. At the very least, it should have a README.md file at the root of the repository. This file provides a high-level overview of the project, guiding new developers or stakeholders on how to set up and use the project. To create a README.md file, use the following command:

```
touch README.md
```

A good README.md file typically includes an introduction to the project, setup instructions, usage examples, and contribution guidelines. Below is an example of what a well-structured README.md may contain:

```
# Project Title

Brief description of the project, its purpose, and high-level goals.

## Getting Started

Instructions to set up the project locally, including prerequisites and installation steps.

\#\#\# Prerequisites

- List of software, libraries, or tools required
- Installation commands

\#\#\# Installation

Step-by-step guide on how to get a development environment running:
```

```
\begin{FittedVerbatim}
command to run the project
\end{FittedVerbatim}

## Usage

Examples and instructions on how to utilize the project effectively.

\begin{FittedVerbatim}
example usage command
\end{FittedVerbatim}

## Contributing

Guidelines for contributing to the project, including code formatting, commit message
    conventions, and the process for submitting pull requests.
```

In addition to the README.md, repositories should contain other key documentation files:

- CONTRIBUTING.md: This file provides specific instructions on how others can contribute to your project. It typically includes coding standards, branch naming conventions, and the process for code reviews.
- CHANGELOG.md: A changelog is crucial for tracking the historical changes made in the project. It documents new features, bug fixes, and any backwards-incompatible changes. The versioning system follows Semantic Versioning (SemVer) principles.
- LICENSE: This file specifies the terms and conditions under which your project's code can be used, modified, and shared. Open-source projects often include licenses such as MIT, Apache 2.0, or GPL.

Maintaining a repository goes beyond just documentation. It also involves keeping the repository clean and well-organized. Some of the best practices include:

Regularly Review and Update Documentation: As the project evolves, so should the documentation. Stale or outdated documentation can mislead developers and lead to integration failures. Automated documentation tools can help keep the documents in sync with the codebase.

Tagging and Releasing: Tag your releases appropriately in Git. Tags mark specific points in your repository's history, like release versions. You can create annotated tags with the following command:

```
git tag -a v1.0 -m "Initial release"
git push origin v1.0
```

Archival of Old Branches: Over time, development branches might become obsolete. To prevent clutter, periodically review and delete or archive old branches. The following commands can be used:

```
git branch -d old-branch # if merged
git branch -D old-branch # if not merged
git push origin --delete old-branch
```

Consistent Branch Naming Conventions: Establish and adhere to branch naming conventions to enhance clarity and consistency. For instance, use prefixes like feature/, fix/, or release/.

Employ Git Hooks: Git hooks are custom scripts that run automatically at various points in the Git workflow, such as committing or pushing. They can enforce coding standards, run tests, and ensure commit messages adhere to a specified format. To add a pre-commit hook:

```
touch .git/hooks/pre-commit
chmod +x .git/hooks/pre-commit
```

Here is an example of a pre-commit hook script:

```
#!/bin/sh
# Example of a simple Git pre-commit hook

# Check for Python syntax errors
find . -name "*.py" | xargs python -m py_compile
if [ $? -ne 0 ]; then
  echo "Python syntax errors were found. Commit aborted."
  exit 1
fi

exit 0
```

Refactoring and Cleaning Code: Incorporate regular intervals to refactor and clean the codebase. Refactoring improves code readability, reduces complexity, and adheres to the "don't repeat yourself" (DRY) principle.

Implementing Continuous Integration (CI): Integrate CI tools like Jenkins, Travis CI, or GitHub Actions to automate the testing and deployment process. These tools run tests on every commit and pull request, ensuring code quality and reducing manual intervention.

Finally, inter-team communication and collaboration can be significantly improved by maintaining well-documented and clean repositories. It ensures that all team members are on the same page and reduces onboarding time for new developers.

Ensuring that your repository documentation is thorough and up-to-date, while systematically organizing and maintaining the repository, will cultivate a robust and efficient development environment. Proper maintenance guarantees that the repository remains a reliable source of truth throughout the software development life cycle.

10.10 Staying Updated with Git Features and Updates

Staying current with Git's latest features and updates is crucial for maintaining an efficient workflow and leveraging new functionalities that can enhance version control practices. Git evolves rapidly, with regular releases introducing improvements, bug fixes, and new capabilities. This section explores strategies and resources for staying updated with Git and ensuring you are proficient in the latest tools it offers.

The first step is to understand the Git release cycle. Git follows a frequent release cadence, typically issuing new versions every two to three months. Each release is meticulously documented, providing detailed information on new features, enhancements, and bug fixes. Monitoring these releases is essential. The official Git website (https://git-scm.com/) and the GitHub repository (https://github.com/git/git) are primary sources for release notes and announcements.

To automatically check for updates and apply them, use package managers. On Debian-based systems such as Ubuntu, the apt tool simplifies this process. For instance, the following commands ensure your system's repositories are up-to-date before upgrading Git:

```
sudo apt update
sudo apt upgrade git
```

On Red Hat-based systems, utilize yum or dnf:

```
sudo yum update git
```

brew is effective for macOS systems:

```
brew update
brew upgrade git
```

Occasionally, you may prefer building Git from source, especially if you require the latest version not yet available in your package manager. The process involves cloning the repository, configuring build parameters, and making the build:

```
git clone https://github.com/git/git.git
cd git
make configure
./configure --prefix=/usr
make all
sudo make install
```

Keeping fiscal awareness of Git's environment is more than just updating software. Incorporating tools and utilities that enhance Git functionalities is also advantageous. For instance, hub, an extension that adds GitHub support to Git on the command level, can be included. Installing hub via brew is straightforward:

```
brew install hub
```

Once installed, verifying the new features is part of the process. Check installed versions and feature lists:

```
git --version
hub --version
```

GitHub Releases offer insight into feature-related discussions and enhancements. Following the official GitHub repositories allows inspection of planned features via milestones and issues. Engaging in these communities not only keeps one updated but also involved in the decision-making processes that shape Git's future.

Subscribing to Git-related newsletters and following relevant forums and blogs are effective strategies. Resources such as the GitHub blog (https://github.blog/), the Git mailing list, and online communities like Stack Overflow provide valuable updates and real-world usage examples. These platforms facilitate discussions regarding lack-of-clarity areas in Git's new features and usage scenarios, bridging the gap between theory and practical implementation.

To further delve into new Git features, thorough comprehension of official documentation is imperative. The Pro Git book, available freely at (https://git-scm.com/book/en/v2), is a foundational resource updated regularly to reflect new features. Exploring this resource and other Git ebooks, tutorials, and courses ensures continuity in learning.

Lastly, enabling experimental features within Git can offer a preview and test of upcoming functionalities. This option can be configured globally or on a per-repository basis, allowing selective testing without affecting stable environments. To enable an experimental feature, such as the sparse-checkout, use the following command:

```
git config --global feature.manyfiles true
```

Test and validate these features within a controlled setup to assess their impact and decide on their applicability to your workflows.

Consider contributing back to the Git community. Sharing usage experiences, providing feedback, and participating in beta tests can significantly influence Git's development direction. Your contributions, no matter how small, ensure that the tool continues to evolve to meet user needs effectively.

Continuous education, vigilant monitoring of release notes, and proactive engagement with the Git community form the cornerstone of staying updated with Git's dynamic feature set. By embracing these practices, you ensure both individuation and organizational proficiency in deploying the latest and most efficient version control methodologies.